John Snell's

WINNING BOWLS

John Snell's

WINNING BOWLS

By John Snell with Bill Pritchard

Souvenir Press

First published in 1982 in Australia by John Currey O'Neil Publishers Pty Ltd
© Bill Pritchard and John Snell

First British Edition published 1983 by Souvenir Press Ltd
43 Great Russell Street London WCIB 3PA
Reprinted 1986

Designed in Australia by Tom Kurema
Printed in Singapore

ISBN 0 285 62584 5

ACKNOWLEDGMENT

The publishers wish to thank The Herald and Weekly Times Limited and Robert Gray of Melbourne, for permission to reproduce photographs.

DEDICATION

To my wife Ricky. Her understanding, sympathy and encouragement are the reasons for my success, which means so much more when shared with someone you love.

Women Bowlers
The bowler throughout this text has been referred to as 'he' purely for convenience. This is in no way intended to exclude or discourage the many women who may wish to take up bowls or who already enjoy the sport. This book is intended equally for both sexes.

CONTENTS

FOREWORD

by David Bryant, C.B.E.

It was at the Banyo Masters Invitation Singles Tournament of 1971 that I first had the pleasure of meeting and competing against John Snell. Even then he was regarded as one of Australia's brightest prospects. I can still recall our most enjoyable match, punctuated by memorable shots and exciting incidents. The large crowd, for the tournament was well supported, appreciated the contest and saw John run out the eventual winner 31-25, after 39 completed ends with seven others killed.

As the event was on a round robin basis as opposed to a knockout, my defeat was not conclusive. By winning the majority of my remaining matches I was adjudged the winner on a superior shot aggregate.

Banyo was my first taste of the Australian tournament scene. In the ensuing months I had time to reflect on what had proved to be an outstanding event played on one of the finest greens that I had encountered. I had been impressed by the skills of my opponents and John Snell figured prominently in my thoughts. His dedicated approach, coupled with his versatile and exciting play were, I considered, to be the very qualities necessary in the making of a great champion. My appraisal proved correct, as his successes over the years speak for themselves.

I have always felt that a champion has to develop complete mastery of the mechanics, has to cultivate deep concentration, and has to possess a superb temperament. These factors, allied to experience gained over the years, breed consistency which should be the aim of every player, whatever his sport. John has all these qualities and in his book endeavours to pass on to the bowler his techniques, his mental approach and the vast experience gained over a long period of highly successful competition.

Many players possess outstanding mechanical skills which are to a degree innate but are only brought to their peak by dedication and constant practice. Mechanical skills form good habits which are far more easily maintained throughout the bowler's playing career as his technique becomes grooved. John is a perfect example of this as he took up the game in his early twenties when his body was still very supple. However, mechanical ability alone is not sufficient to make a top class player and it is his mastery of the other ingredients that makes John a great champion.

I have always considered that bowls requires the highest degree of self-discipline and a methodical approach. Every delivery requires the utmost concentration and it is in this department I feel John's strength lies. From the moment he steps on the mat, the thought and care that he puts into every delivery is an object lesson for very young and old bowlers alike. His will to make every bowl count makes for greater consistency and results in a far lower percentage of loose deliveries.

All sports have their various fascinations. The beauty of the game of bowls, as is often stated by players throughout the world, is that no two greens are alike. In every country conditions vary considerably, and when one moves from hemisphere to hemisphere one encounters the extremes. Bowls played on the holding surfaces of the northern hemisphere requires completely different tactics from those employed on the ultra fast surfaces found in New Zealand and Australia. Adapting to new conditions requires an analytical mind and a complete understanding of technique, which in turn relies upon a sound tactical ability.

John regards every game as a challenge and when encountering conditions unfamiliar to him he adapts quickly, which proves that his game is based upon a strong foundation with the correct mental approach. His two excursions to the slower greens in Edmonton, Canada and Worthing, England resulted in him taking home two silver medals, which underlines his versatility. Competing against the world's top players he showed that he was able to produce 'the goods' and proved that he was adaptable to all conditions.

Having met and played against John on several occasions since that day at Banyo, fifteen years ago, I can thoroughly recommend that any bowler will benefit from reading his book. The contents are based on a sound knowledge of the game which has been gained by deep thought and an experience acquired over many years of the highest competitive play. Although having been highly successful in team events I tend to think of John as one of the world's outstanding singles players. His career has been similar in many ways to my own, in that his successes in team play are perhaps overshadowed by his many single-handed successes. As he is a perfectionist, the challenge of tightening his game probably made him concentrate on singles. I personally feel one can achieve a higher degree of rhythm and touch and a greater satisfaction in this type of competition.

Being a champion is, I suppose, every bowler's ambition, but having the temperament to reach this height is another thing. Like other champions John is calm, cool and collected, with that very necessary 'killer instinct', but where he gains admiration of all other players is that he is the perfect gentleman both on and off the green. I regularly make the statement that it is not necessary to display undesirable emotions or resort to ungentlemanly conduct in order to win, and if a player shows any of these qualities it is a breach of self-discipline.

Good sportsmanship and good manners cost nothing and John's philosophy and good name are appreciated throughout the bowling world. I am sure this means more to him than his numerous successes on the green. Being a good ambassador for the game and one's country is of the utmost importance and the many spectators who witnessed and were thrilled by his spectacular play in the Kodak Masters at Worthing during 1982 will, I am sure, echo my sentiments. May his successes continue.

THE FIRST QUESTION

1

There was a time, not too long ago, when sport was played for fun and recreation. Now, few sportsmen think in those terms. If they do, then their thoughts are sure to be drowned out by the loudest sound heard anywhere in the sporting world, that of the cash register.

Consider the golfer who has just missed a metre putt. He looks miserable and no wonder — the mistake could have cost him $50 000 or more. For the same reason John McEnroe argues the call and insults the line umpire; and the crowd screams for the blood of both.

You have seen it and so have I, because television, plus sponsorship, have turned golf, tennis, cricket and football into a giant world-wide entertainment industry. This is sport in the 1980s and for many decades to come.

Or, is it?

It seems that, at least in the older generation, there is a natural regret for the passing of the old ways — a longing for sport the way it was. And yet it is beginning to look as if one of the most remarkable periods in any sport is about to burst on the game with the oldest participants of all.

Lawn bowls is now being exposed to sponsorship and television — it, too, has much to offer a wider world: all the things that make for good sport. There is success, and failure, comedy, tragedy, suspense, skill, concentration and stamina and the one quality so absent from other sports these days. It is called sportsmanship.

To me, watching the rush of events in the game since the World Bowls Championships were held in Australia early in 1980, has been a matter of some pleasure and satisfaction. Yet, basically, the game has hardly changed at all. It still gives and demands as much as it ever did. It allows one to obtain as much enjoyment and exercise as the effort required to play.

That old nonsense about bowls being a pastime only for the retired is being laid to rest by the numbers of young men to be found on the bowling greens of Australia. To them and to you, the reader, I want to ask a simple question.

Do you want to be a winner at bowls? Saying yes is easy. The hard part comes in finding the real answer, for it lies deep within yourself. Read this book, take its contents to your heart and your mind, let me guide you and then you may find not only the answer but also something new about yourself.

If you do these things, you will play winning bowls. Somewhere along the way, all champions in all sports reached those higher peaks by unlocking the great reserves of confidence, concentration and tenacity that are in us all. The key is a burning desire to be better than we are. This is the basis for my belief that champions are made and not born.

I can show you the way to greater things in bowls, whether you are a newcomer or an advanced player. It is a remarkable thing about the sport of bowls that a man can win a title within a few years of taking it up, or many years later. Many have done both. I cannot think of any greater illustration of this point than the remarkable R. T. (Dick) Harrison. He served in the Boer War, took up bowls in 1903, and won the Victorian singles title three years later, and the State Champion of Champions title the following year. In 1943, thirty-six years later, Dick Harrison again won that Champion of Champions title. He was then seventy years of age.

A champion requires dedication and desire greater than most people's understanding. Yet, in these pages, I can set you on the road to that understanding and show you the physical and mental skills and techniques you will need. These may not be of great importance to the 'social' bowler, and why should they be? After all, it is part of the game's enjoyment that nobody really cares too deeply about who wins or loses in a social game.

At the higher levels, however, it's a different story, and the psychology of lawn bowls assumes an essential part of a champion's game. I call it the 'inner game' and to play it, a bowler needs to understand what has to be done and why; how it can be done better; and most of all, how to build within himself the confidence and will to win.

In any sport, the basic and most important factor is the attitude of the player himself. If the attitude is right, then the benefits to be obtained become almost automatic.

'Why didn't I take up bowls twenty years ago?' is more a comment than a question and one I've heard a thousand times from bowlers who began only after they had retired. Most of them did not start earlier because their attitude was wrong. They had been led to believe that old myth about bowls being an old man's game.

Whoever described bowls, more accurately, as a young man's game that old men can also play, knew a thing or two. Whatever your age, it can teach you the twin arts of relaxation and concentration like no other sport. It is also a great leveller. I recall that after winning my first club championship, I was invited to captain a team of four at the start of the following season. Still fired with confidence and enthusiasm from my championship, and keen to do well as a skipper, I approached the first match with great expectations. Then came the thud. Not only were we beaten, we didn't even register on the scoreboard!

Bowlers, generally, can be fitted into one of three groups, each producing a great deal of enjoyment in different ways.

First, there is the social bowler who plays only for the pleasure of it. He likes to win, but if he loses, he hardly gives a thought as to why he lost.

The second group is made up of competitors, who play socially but in addition, relish pennant matches and club tournaments. They usually spend a great deal of time aimlessly practising and playing, but seldom critically examine their game. Nor are they dedicated enough to make the sacrifices necessary to move into the next group.

Only a minority of bowlers can claim membership of the third level. It comprises champions and potential champions who get there through dedication, hard work and sacrifice. They have a burning desire to succeed and an analytical and self-critical mind that allows them to sort out what is right and what is wrong with their game and their approach.

Now which group is for you?

If your ambitions take you no further than the first or second rungs, you are certain to reap great enjoyment and make many friendships from your efforts.

If, however, you see yourself in the third group, the best of the best, then the struggle will be greater. But, so too will be the rewards, mentally and physically.

The decision is yours.

THE BANKER FROM THE BUSH

2

Is the world of sports merely a world of dreams? Possibly, yet dreams are not always foolish and sometimes they can become goals. Mine did, and over the last twenty years or so, I've had the great good fortune to have achieved most of them.

As a boy I often dreamed (as boys do) of being a champion, at anything; and in those years just after the Second World War, there was plenty of material around to feed such ideals.

I was born at Jerilderie, New South Wales, in 1934, in the middle of the Great Depression. Three years later, my family moved to the Murray River township of Mathoura and set up house across the road from the public tennis courts and the local football oval. My father, Syd, was a keen sportsman — still is, for that matter — and was well-known around Mathoura for his prowess at tennis, cricket, football and billiards. Life in a bush town was pretty good for a young nipper in those days, and while my parents were not all that strict, they made sure I wasn't going to misspend my youth in Mathoura's billiards parlour. Nevertheless, from time to time, I was able to sneak a look through the yellowed windows at Dad, my idol, in action at the tables.

With such a mentor, I soon became sports-mad, and showed promise at most of those I took up. It didn't stop on the playing fields — any sporting book, magazine or newspaper article I could lay my hands on would be read and reread. On reflection, my desire to analyse all sorts of sports, games and those who played them goes back to those days.

Mathoura did pretty well in the district cricket and football competitions, despite its population of less than 1000, so it was with great pride that at the age of thirteen,

I was selected in the town's senior football side. It could hardly have been for my size, weighing in as I did at 45 kilograms (7 st. 2 lbs). Next, I was chosen for Mathoura's cricket team.

Between school, family, cricket and football, there didn't seem much time for anything else. But there was tennis, just across the road, and soon the other sports were being pushed into the background.

Tennis produced my first firm thoughts about the future. I wanted to be a champion and to play Davis Cup for Australia. By 1951 we had Hoad and Rosewall, Sedgman and McGregor, and when in that year I was chosen to join a squad of young hopefuls being coached by that tough old task-master, Harry Hopman, I thought I was on my way. My first day in the squad was awful. After hitting only two balls, Hopman called me to the net. 'Son', he said, 'do you know that your reflexes are abnormally slow?' My father had mentioned this on several occasions, but when Harry Hopman spelled it out, well that was that — no Davis Cup for John Snell. But there was my career with the Westpac Bank to think about and my late teens and early twenties settled into a succession of postings to country towns around Victoria.

With marriage, work, tennis and my latest discovery, golf, life was again full. It took me until 1960 to find one sport where slow reflexes did not inhibit my progress. The way things turned out, I was fortunate to have taken up bowls at the age of twenty-five, which was extremely young for a bowler in those days. The early taste of bowls sparked that dream of mine, to become a champion sportsman. It came in such a natural, unconscious way, that I am puzzled why newspaper people make such a thing of it.

The bank had transferred me to Kaniva, a small wheat town in Victoria's Wimmera, not very different from so many others in the area. Lack of competition on the tennis court and the constant interruptions to life's routines through bank postings, had caused my interest in tennis to fall away. In Kaniva the tennis courts happened to be right alongside the town's bowling green. I had known a little about the game from staying with my uncle at Echuca, and at Kaniva I began to spend a bit of time hanging over the fence, waiting for a set of tennis, and watching the bowls. A casual invitation one day to try my hand around a bowl was enough to make me jump that fence.

I realised pretty quickly, as do most bowlers, that not only was bowls much harder than it looked, but it was also a sport in which to become absorbed. I worked hard at my fitness and my game and determined to become as good as I could. Twenty-six years on, and nothing has changed.

But more of that later. Kaniva was the start but in 1961 it was time for another bank posting, this time to Heywood in Victoria's Western District. Whether or not fate was taking a hand I don't know, but it was at Heywood that I met a most remarkable man who was to play a big part in shaping my approach to bowls — Gordon Langdon. Gordon saw nothing special in himself, but others did, and they never doubted his guts and determination, in learning to play left-handed after losing the use of his right arm. Gordon was a great inspiration to me and I learned much from playing with and against him, especially in his two defeats of me in the club singles championships of 1962 and

1963. In later years, I had the pleasure of playing in his Victorian team where he impressed me as one of the best draw-shot bowlers I had seen.

My first club championship came two years later with a transfer to Ararat. If there was a real turnaround in my career, it came at Ararat and not Kaniva. That championship made me realise that to get anywhere, in bowls and in life, one must have a set of real goals, and not merely dreams. I set mine, both long and short term: nothing less than the best in the world, and along the way, the best in Victoria, then Australia. All this meant sacrifice and dedication. Much to my wife Ricky's concern, I spent many of my leisure hours practising and analysing the game, as well as the style and tactics of the top bowlers in the district. But Ararat also brought me the thing I most wanted. In 1966, in a successful defence of the club championship, Ricky came to watch me play for the first time, and gradually, from that point, her bewilderment turned to support for what I was trying to do.

With hindsight, it is strange how the shape of my bowls career was governed by my bank postings. From Ararat, the next took me to Corryong and with it, a promotion, although it didn't seem that way at the time. Corryong is a delightful town, nestling in the Snowy Mountains of north eastern Victoria. It is cold country, with snow and a short bowling season and because it was so far from anywhere, the Corryong Club didn't have a pennant team. It was virtually social bowls only, which was enough of a challenge to make me spend hours in lonely practice. When in 1968 I appeared in Melbourne during my annual holidays, to play in the Victorian Masters title, I threatened nothing and no one. I had no pressure on me, because I wasn't expected to survive the first round, let alone win the title.

In almost every match I had to come from behind and in the final, it was the same, winning with the last bowl of the last end.

What a dream way to win my first major title!

Oddly enough, when I went back and won again the following year, there was still no pressure. Nobody had ever won the Masters twice, let alone two consecutively. It was enough to secure my next goal — to play for Victoria. Those three years at Corryong, it seems, were significant ones for they saw me on my way to success, despite the lack of competitive bowls in the district. In fact, this period threw me back on my own resources and the conditions there of slow, heavy and often wet greens, forced me to change my style.

After nine years in the game, I found myself playing for Victoria with my sights now set on representing Australia. Victoria nominated me for a place in the national team for the 1970 Commonwealth Games in Scotland, the 1972 World Championships in England, the 1974 Games in Christchurch and the 1976 World titles in South Africa. I stayed at home for them all. Then in 1978 came the green and gold blazer I had so long sought. That trip to Canada earned me a silver medal in the singles, as did the 1980 World Championships at Frankston. Each time, David Bryant proved himself, as he has done so often, to be the best in the world. Nevertheless, there is still time for that one remaining goal to be mine.

When one looks at it, the sport of lawn bowls has been virtually standing still for more than 100 years. Certainly, there have been changes, but they have been small and sometimes hardly perceptible. Tradition, one of the game's finest attributes, has in the past been treated with too much respect, proving a barrier to real change in the way bowls has been promoted. As it has happened, change has been imposed from outside and the spark has been provided by the television coverage of the 1980 World Championships and other events since then, as well as by the television series, *Jack High*. Television has whetted people's appetites for bowls and shown that it is a real contest and not merely a pastime.

I believe the sport stands now where tennis stood twenty years ago, facing the onset of an 'open' or professional game. It is a time for new blood and particularly new champions, which is one of the reasons for writing this book. If it helps bring in that new blood, or in some small way, contributes to the making of even one new champion, then to some extent I will have repaid the game for the rewards it has given me.

Differing circumstances, and physical and mental make-up, make it impossible for everyone to follow my 'beginner to master' plan. But with a similar approach to short and long term goals, and with determination and application, anyone can make it.

I like Thomas Edison's famous dictum which to me sums it all up: 'Genius is one per cent inspiration, and ninety-nine per cent perspiration'.

THE BEGINNING

3

Of course, we all know that bowls is only a game.

One man crouches, swings his arm and sets in motion a bowl weighing 1.5 kilograms. It travels over clipped grass in an arc for 24 metres or more towards a little white ball. His opponent then does the same. It can go on for hours.

Well, so much for the fiction. J. B. Priestley put paid to that sort of thinking in sport when he wrote that to describe Soccer as twenty-two hirelings kicking a ball is 'merely to say that a violin is wood and catgut, that *Hamlet* is just so much ink and paper'.

It may be that lawn bowls started out as just a game. But it is now much more. It has soul, subtlety and character, although the basics certainly are simple enough.

Anyone wanting to take up the game, either for friendship, competition or both, has only to drop into a club. He will be made welcome and will probably be invited to join. But give the matter a little thought; select a club near your home or between work and home so that you can call in for regular practice during the week.

From the club secretary you will learn about the club, your part in it, what to wear and how much it will cost you to play. Having made the decision to join, the club coach or a senior player will be assigned to look after you and show you the ropes, and more importantly, the rudiments of the game. They are relatively easy to grasp.

In singles the player who wins the toss of the coin, rolls the jack to the other end of the green. It must travel at least 20 metres. Then bowling alternately, each player delivers four bowls. The player whose bowl finishes nearest the jack, scores one. If his second is also closer than his opponent's nearest, he scores two. And so on. In pairs each player delivers four bowls, in triples, three and in fours, two.

Having joined a club, where to from there?

The Chinese, as always, have a proverb that fits the situation. It says that a journey of a thousand miles begins with but a single step. On the road to the top in bowls, you have just taken that step. The next is to outfit yourself for the encounters to come.

SELECTING YOUR BOWLS

In choosing your weapons, go for the largest bowls you can most comfortably hold. They need less effort to deliver, which means a smoother swing and consequently, fewer problems at the other end. Also, in a measure for shot, the difference between winning and losing can be the difference between a large bowl and a small one.

Bowls come in sizes numbered 0 to 7, with just a centimetre's difference between the diameters of the bowls at each end of the scale.

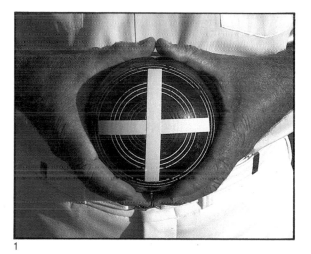

1

As a guide to the correct size for you, clamp your hands around the running surface of a large bowl[1]. The tips of your longest fingers should touch, as should your thumb nails. If they don't, then try the next size down and so on, until you find the bowl size which suits. As I said, a large bowl is generally better than a small bowl; but if you have small hands, and feel at a disadvantage, there are ways to overcome the problem. One is to exercise your hands by pushing the top halves of your fingers and thumb of one hand against those on the other. In my first seven or eight years of bowls, I exercised like this constantly and increased my hand-span by two centimetres.

If your span is limited, another method is to experiment with the grips discussed later in this chapter.

The matter of bowls selection is really in two parts. We have dealt with size. Now let us look at weight.

Each size bowl comes in two weights: medium and heavy. The one you choose should again be governed by comfort, but remember these points.

- *WIND* — A heavyweight of any size is less affected than its medium counterpart in windy conditions. For example, a heavyweight will usually turn more into a cross-breeze, and less with it, in the last two metres of running than a mediumweight.
- *GREENS* — In Australia's southern states where greens tend to be heavier and more lush, especially before Christmas, a heavyweight bowl tends to sit down more in the grass. This creates more friction on the bowl as it runs; thus you need to put more effort into the act of delivery. It may be only a slight effort, but it could be enough to upset your rhythm and balance. On the other hand, Queensland's greens, for example, are faster than those down south and the

heavyweight does not require the same amount of energy. Remember too, that it is less affected by the wind.

Some bowlers have had success with different sets of bowls for different conditions. However I don't believe in this approach and make it a rule to keep only one set in the house. It removes the temptation to chop and change. With two or more sets, it is too easy to find excuses for poor play by telling yourself that you used the wrong bowls on the day. Switching weights, I find, also creates difficulties in judging rhythm and finish.

To sum up, select the largest sized bowl you can handle comfortably.

If most of your play is to be on greens such as those in the south of the country, choose mediumweights; if in the north, on the faster greens, heavyweights could be the answer.

Which ever your decision, stick with it.

THE GRIP (Forehand)

In most sports, your grip on your equipment governs how you will perform with it. Lawn bowls is no different and the starting point for a smooth, successful delivery is the grip on the bowl.

The enemy of the smooth delivery is the wobble. On a windy day, wobble can kill your line and draw stone dead within two metres of the bowl leaving your hand. On my bowls, you will notice white lines. I've painted them on the rings to tell me the instant after delivery if the bowl is wobbling. If it is, then the grip requires correction.

The right way is to place your middle finger on the centre of the bowl's running surface[2]. Bring your other fingers close together alongside, if you can. I can't because of a broken finger suffered many years ago. If you have a similar difficulty, do

2

4

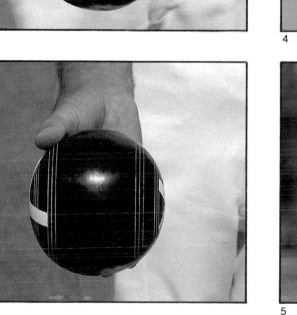

3

5

try to keep your fingers as close together as possible.

The thumb should be held in a comfortable position near the large ring on the bowl, but without exerting too much pressure[3]. Holding the thumb down hard only increases the likelihood of the bowl wobbling. The thumb is used more as a steadier. Now, with the bowl sitting on your four fingers, [4,5] there should be a straight line from the running surface, up your arm to the shoulder. The wrist must not be cocked;

for one thing it is not natural. The hand is not a straight extension of the arm, but normally points away at a slight angle. If you try to keep the hand straight, I promise you nothing more than bad deliveries, a tired wrist and a case of tension at the end of the day. A cocked wrist is against all the principles of relaxation, which is one of the secrets of winning bowls.

Always before a delivery, check your grip. If it is not right, step off the mat and start again.

ON THE MAT

4

YOUR FEET

It is often asserted, simplistically perhaps, that 'style' or 'class' distinguishes a champion.

Maybe. I've known a few bowlers, very smooth, very classy-looking, but I wouldn't count on them to produce the goods. On the other hand, there are others who look very ordinary, but who always get the results on the board. That they do so is usually the end-product of a lot of hard work and above all, concentration and application. Where it all pays off is on the mat.

When a bowler stands there ready to deliver, his mind is active and alert, check-listing what he is doing. Or, at least it should be. Yet, thousands of players merely step onto the mat, without thought and with almost indecent haste. Their bowls are launched with the same abandon. Is it any wonder that this vast army will never gain the rewards of good bowling?

Any student of the game will tell you that eighty per cent of the work of delivering a bowl smoothly and successfully is done before a foot is placed on the mat. The top bowler has thought out beforehand what he is going to do, and how. That ability does not come naturally. Learn it all now and you won't have to break yourself of bad habits later on.

The first step is to place your feet correctly. They will determine the line your bowl will take up the green and to a great extent, how it will finish.

If you are left-handed, do in reverse all that follows.

I prefer to bowl from the inside of the mat. For a forehand shot I stand as near to the left-hand edge of the mat as the rules will allow[1]. Remember that the back foot, when you deliver, must be on or over the mat. For a backhand delivery, the position is as near

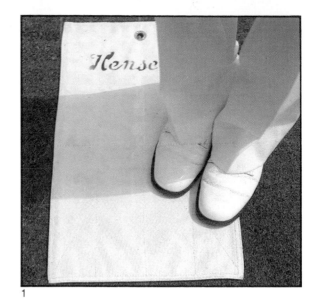
1

to the right-hand edge as possible[2]. For both shots the right heel is against the edge of the mat. This allows you to deliver along the narrowest possible line of the green. If for example, your opponent is playing from the centre of the mat, then your line of delivery is about 15 centimetres (6 inches) inside his line. There are three advantages in this method.

1 It gives you a psychological edge in that it is likely to worry an opponent who thinks he bowls narrow anyway.

2 You are making use of the worn part of the green, that is, the strip where the most play has taken place and where bowlers walk when changing ends. This helps to reduce friction on the bowl as it travels and keeps it away from the relatively unused area. That new grass can make

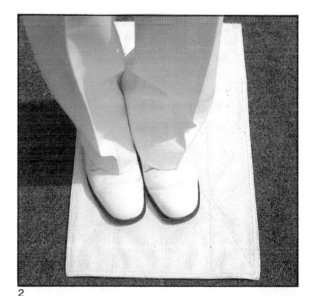
2

the bowl stand out and make it harder to draw in to the jack.

3   With your right heel always against the edge of the mat, it is easier to keep the same line for each delivery. You know your position on the mat at all times, which helps to produce consistency — the essence of good bowls.

A good example of the way in which this method can work, came my way a few years ago during a club championship match at Geelong, in Victoria. The green had not been cut for two days and had a fair growth of grass. I bowled inside my opponent's line and, as the match wore on, the centre of the rink became more flattened. While I was able to consistently outdraw him, his bowls became too narrow, ran across the head or tracked into the new grass and stayed out. The result was that he became increasingly frustrated, lost his rhythm and the match.

GETTING YOUR LINE

In the next chapter, I'll show you how to find your aiming point at the other end of the green. Right now we come to the second step in placing your feet correctly.

1   Step onto the mat with your right heel against the edge and the toe pointing directly along the line you intend to bowl.

2   Bring your left foot up and parallel with the other, but leave a gap of about one centimetre (a quarter inch). Jamming your feet together could cramp your delivery.

3   The left toecap should also be about three centimetres in front of the right. This has the effect of tucking your right hip slightly back and out of the way for a free delivery swing.

THE STANCE

Watch a game of bowls at any club in Australia and you will see as many different styles on the mat as there are players. Some resemble a praying mantis, others appear to be suffering from indigestion, while many look so off-balance that a puff of wind would pitch them forward.

I've always been a supporter of the upright or athletic stance, but experience has taught me that you must bend at the waist. An angle of 70-80 degrees is sufficient[3]. This starts you on your way down with balance, and enables you to get right behind the delivery. It may seem a little strange at first, but plenty of practice will make it second nature.

In addition, bend your knees a little, but keep them relaxed, maintaining more weight on the right foot than on the left[4]. You are then better placed to transfer your weight in stepping forward, making for a smoother delivery.

Now check to see that your shoulders are square[5]. They're not? Well, there's a simple way to ensure that they are square, facing your line of delivery.

Some coaches advocate that you steady the bowl with your free hand. I don't; I believe this tends to drag your left shoulder out of line just before delivery. My approach is to use my left hand to steady my bowling arm[6]; touching near the elbow, yet still enabling the shoulders to remain square. Over the years, I've noticed that other top bowlers use the same or similar techniques, such as placing their left hands on their left knees. Whatever method they use, their shoulders remain square.

Early in my career I developed a bad habit, one that haunts a large percentage of bowlers. Instead of holding the bowl out to the side of my body, giving me a clear swing, I held it straight out in front. This meant the

3

swing had to follow an arc to get around my body, resulting in inconsistent deliveries. So I devised the technique of pushing my right elbow out with my left hand to a point where it was clear of my body. It now seems to have become a trademark.

To sum up:

1 Get your feet right on the mat. Your right foot should point along the delivery line, the left foot parallel to it and slightly in front.

2 The stance should be fairly upright, but the body bent at the waist at an angle of 70-80 degrees.

3 The knees should be slightly bent and the shoulders square, the bowl held to the side and not out in front of the body.

4

5

6

7A   7B   7C

ELEVATION

Clearly, when it comes to putting together all parts of your stance, each is just as important as the other. One cannot work properly without the others, and the final component, which takes you to the point of delivery, concerns what is known as 'elevation'.

Briefly, this means the position of your bowling arm. Look again at the photographs of my stance and you will notice that the arm is slightly below a line parallel with the ground. With the bowl starting the backswing from this height, I will have the correct amount of momentum to deliver the bowl to the speed of that particular green.

On a slow or heavy surface or on a long end, you have to propel the bowl much faster than you would on a fast or slick green. To do this you elevate your arm so that a natural swing will take your bowl back further and then forward faster.

On a fast green or a short end, you need far less effort, so the arm is held at waist height or lower. Finding the exact position is a matter of judgment and experience, both of which you can gain only by constant practice and play on all types of greens.

THE DELIVERY

You are now ready to get that bowl moving. The action necessary is a natural follow-on to the stance you have taken up on the mat. The first few thousand deliveries will need all your concentration. After that the delivery will be completely natural.

There are two essentials:

1 Rhythm

2 A long follow-through, even to the point of exaggeration. This is where many bowlers fall down on the job in the last stride.

7D   7E   7F

Rhythm is produced by co-ordinating your step forward with the start of your backswing[7A]. Remember that in your stance, there should be more weight on the right foot than on the left, so that your weight will transfer smoothly[7B]. I tend to step later than most but it doesn't concern me as it enables me to transfer weight later and get more body weight into the shot.

Move the left foot forward and place it firmly and flatly on the ground[7C]. The length of the step should be about that of a normal walking pace: 75 centimetres or 30 inches. Anything shorter will cramp your style and delivery; anything longer and you'll overbalance.

As you start moving your foot, you begin moving the upper half of your body down and the arm back, all in one movement[7D]. The arm comes back to a point between 30 and 40 centimetres (12 to 16 inches) behind your leg[7E]. The entire action must be deliberate, not jerky. Sometimes you may have to quicken it up on a heavy green, slow it down on a fast green. Above all, be smooth.

On the forward swing the bowl is released about 20 centimetres (8 inches) in front of your left foot. At that point, your right knee will be almost touching your left ankle and about 10 centimetres (4 inches) above the ground[7F]. Your free hand should rest on your left knee. If you have done all that, then you know that you have got right down to the job and put the bowl to ground smoothly without a trace of bump or wobble.

7G

FOLLOW-THROUGH

As you release the bowl, the arm continues to swing through the line, generating the pace needed for the shot played. It is almost guaranteed by pushing the arm out in an exaggerated follow-through[7G]. Reach out, in this action, as if you were trying to grasp the aiming mark at the other end of the green. If you can feel a stretch in your shoulder, then you have carried out the follow-through correctly. Finally, end the whole movement with the palm of your hand facing upwards and stay there until the bowl has travelled a third of the way up the green.

The action is always the same when you are drawing to the jack, whether the shot is on the forehand or on the backhand. On the latter, the only things you do differently are to stand facing your delivery line on the backhand, and to turn your bowl over so that the small centre disc is facing inwards. To emphasise all the points in the delivery action, the accompanying photographs are of the backhand draw shot.[8A-F]

Be smooth, deliberate and have rhythm in your action and always finish with that exaggerated follow-through, palm upwards.

The payoff will come at the other end of the green when your bowl comes to rest against that little white jack!

8A

8B

8C

8D

8E

8F

ON TARGET

5

ROLLING THE JACK

In a sport demanding so much concentration and application, it is curious that one of the most obvious fundamentals of bowls is so often overlooked. The simple act of rolling the jack to start a match or an end, seems to be widely regarded as hardly worthy of attention. It is the jack which controls much of the game, yet I suppose that about eighty per cent of bowlers toss it down without thought or care.

Supposing a skipper in a fours match wishes to change the length, and his leader, whose job it is, cannot roll the jack to that length, the whole team's tactics and play could be disrupted.

By the same token, a singles player who cannot roll the jack with accuracy might have thrown his whole game plan.

Under Australian bowls laws, there are two things to remember about the jack. After being rolled, it must finish at least 20 metres from the mat and it must come to rest inside the boundaries of the rink. If the length is less than 20 metres, then you could be challenged and the jack handed to your opponent. The same happens if it rolls into the ditch or over the boundary line. Either way, you have handed control of the length to your opponent, and that is just carelessness.

Logically, it pays to develop the ability, through practice, to roll the jack with care and accuracy. The starting point for this is the grip.

There are many ways to hold the jack. Here I have illustrated just three of them. Two[1A-B] are wrong, yet they can be seen being used on greens all over Australia every week. The correct grip[1C] on the jack is just as important as that on the bowl.

1A

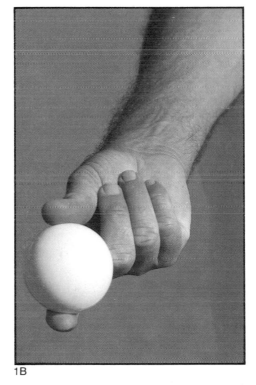
1B

1C

Study the next photograph[1D]. It shows the correct grip — cupping the jack in your fingers as you would a bowl with the thumb placed not too firmly on the top. The hand and arm must be relaxed.

The delivery is the same as that for your bowl, the only difference being where you place your feet.

Stand square on the left side of the mat[2] so that you deliver the jack straight down the centre line. As you stand, fix in your mind's eye where you mean the jack to finish and remember that being smaller and lighter, it requires far less momentum than a bowl. Follow-through in exactly the same way as you would in delivering a bowl. It can give you a 'feel' for the bowl to follow.

1D

THE AIMING POINT

On the face of it, the hardest part in delivering a bowl with accuracy seems to lie in choosing the arc it must follow to the target. That is understandable, for not only is the bowl elliptical or biassed, it will also be affected in its travel by the weather, the green, or both.

Greens vary from one to another, as do rinks within a green, while one side of a rink can play differently from the other. A bowl may take a wider arc on one hand and a narrow one on the other. In early summer, a green may play quite differently from two months later. As it dries out, or when the atmosphere is overcast and humid, or, as evening falls, the effect grass has on a bowl will alter. A green in Queensland may play faster and wider than one in Victoria at the same time of the year. The point is that whatever the conditions, you must be alert to any change in them.

Clearly, judgment plays a part in choosing the path your bowl must take. Just how much judgment is involved is a moot point, and some bowlers approach the whole business on a 'suck it and see' basis. I'm afraid that method is too inexact for me, and it should be for you, too, if you want to be more than just mediocre at the game. By all means, use the trial ends before a match to judge how the green is playing and, if need be, continue to do this during the first few ends of the game.

Once you have an idea of the green conditions and the width of arc your bowl must take on both sides of the rink, you can then use one of two techniques to ensure that each bowl you deliver is accurate. In fact, you may use both because the methods complement each other. The important thing to remember is to take your time and get it right with each and every delivery. Both methods begin before you step onto the mat.

Here are the main points to remember:

1 Visualise the arc or path you want the bowl to take and fix it in your mind, together with the length of the jack.

2 Remember the feet placements from the previous chapter? Step onto the mat and place your right foot in line with the path you have visualised. Keep that position in your mind because later, you can adjust your toe to give a wider or narrower line if the pace of the green changes or if the jack is shifted off the centre line during play.

3 Now choose an imaginary point along the visualised line where the bowl should begin to turn in towards the jack. This is called the 'shoulder' of the green and it is your aiming point. This is one method of getting your line. The second is the one which I use and as I have said, is really an extension of the first.

4 Having picked out the shoulder, continue the imaginary line to the bank of the green. There, choose a suitable visual mark and use this as your aiming point. In this illustration[3A] the mark has been added for identification, but it could be a peg, a painted mark or even the leg of a seat. Be sure though, that it is not an object someone may move during a game. You will notice that my head is up, indicating that I am sighting on the aiming point, and that my right foot is pointing up the path I intend to bowl.

5 As you begin the delivery action, your head goes down[3B] with your body and your eyes come back down that imaginary line to a point on the green

3A

3B

about five metres in front of the mat. As in hitting a golf ball, it is important to get your eyes down onto that spot as you deliver. It has the effect of getting your head down. Lift it at the moment of delivery and you will probably dump the bowl and ruin the whole sequence.

The bowl delivered in these photographs, finished about a metre wide of the jack on a green running at twelve-and-a-half seconds. To correct for the next shot, the aiming mark has to come in along the bank towards the jack for a distance of about two-thirds of a metre.

4A

4B

The important thing to remember about this technique of targetting, is that when the mat is shifted, either up or down the green, so too will your aiming point have to alter. For example, as the mat is moved forward, your aiming mark will shift closer to the centre line. Here[4A], the mat has been moved 3.5 metres up the green.

I have brought my aiming mark in towards the jack about three-quarters of a metre, which I judge to be about right. Again my head has come down[4B], my eyes returning along the imaginary line to a point about five metres in front of the mat as I deliver.

This method of aiming is more precise than merely guessing the arc of the bowl or,

in bowls terms, the amount of grass it will take. The advantage is that you will always have your original mark from which to make adjustments. This is most helpful when playing on fast greens where, at times, your mark on the bank could be 8 or 10 metres along from the centre of your rink.

By the way, don't fall for the trap of sighting on a moveable object. One bowler I know made the mistake of using as his aiming point a bowls bag sitting on the bank. He only realised when the game was over that somebody had moved it!

That last bowl in the photographs, incidentally, finished where it was intended — right on the jack.

JACK SHIFTED — NEW AIMING POINTS

This is where we become technical — how to cope with a jack which has been shifted by a bowl in play from the centre line to the boundary line of the rink.

The subject is worthy of some study as the situation is a common one in bowls. If you can rise to the situation, say in competition, then you have added another weapon to your armoury.

In finding the new, correct arc or path for your bowl[5], you *do not* judge the distance between the number (A) and the aiming point (B), then extend that out the same distance towards (C).

The correct method is to imagine a line at 90 degrees to your original aiming point, drawn from the number (A), crossing the original aiming line (E) and extending out by the same distance between (A) and (E). This will give you the correct line (D) which, extended to the bank, gives you the new aiming point (C).

Simple? Well perhaps it doesn't seem that way, but you will find that experience will teach you to calculate the new line in a matter of seconds.

In the example it is assumed that the green is perfect, and the surface is completely level. Unfortunately greens seldom are that way, and usually are slower out near the boundary line because the grass hasn't been used so much. The aiming point for a shot like this will therefore, be slightly more narrow than point (D).

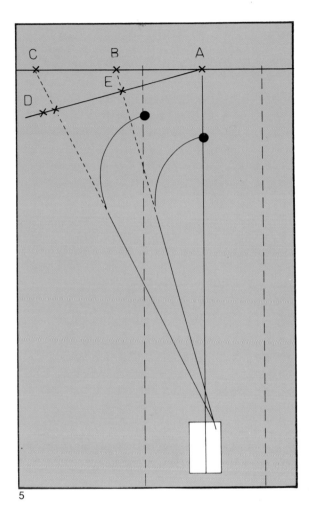

5

AVOIDING TROUBLE

One of the biggest problems some bowlers have is in avoiding a bowl in their draw. In other words, a previously delivered bowl (usually an opponent's) which has come to a stop short of the jack and directly in the arc or path leading to it.

The danger as they see it, is in knocking up or promoting the opponent's bowl closer to the jack and perhaps making it shot. The problem is mostly in their own minds and one of two things happen. Either they change to the other hand, say from forehand to backhand, and probably deliver a wasted bowl that finishes nowhere useful, or because they see the bowl to be bigger than it really is, their own is drawn to it like a magnet and *it is* knocked in for shot.

Here's how to get around the problem.

You can choose to go either inside or outside the bowl in the draw, which, in this illustration is on the forehand. Always use the mat to give you a slightly different arc to clear the bowl. Here[6], the new position for the feet is on the *outside* of the mat.

The green is slow, the grass not having been cut for forty-eight hours. The opposition bowl, (indicated by the white broken line[7]) has stopped in the forehand draw. The yellow broken line shows the new line and aiming point from the right hand side of the mat. Add to the shift in feet placement an increased pace to the bowl of about two-thirds of a metre, and the shot should not only clear the opponent's bowl, but also draw in for shot a few centimetres behind the jack.

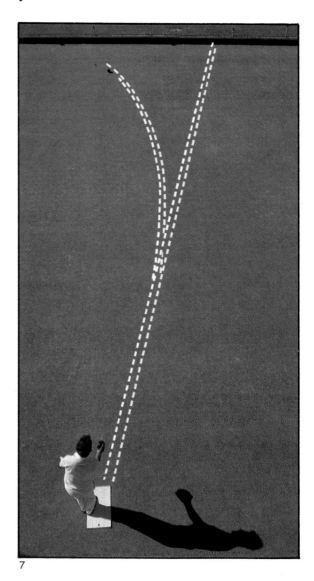

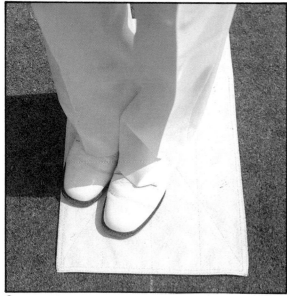

6

7

For a similar problem on the backhand, the same points apply, except that the feet are moved to the extreme left of the mat[8].

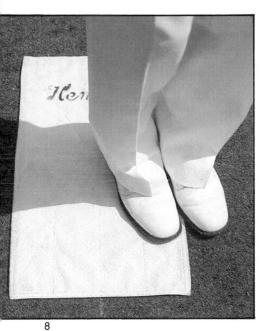

8

This new position for the feet provides the most advantageous arc or angle for the bowl to clear the opponent's shot lying directly in the path to the jack.

Again the white broken line[9] shows the path of the opposition bowl, and the yellow one illustrates the angle needed to clear it and draw the shot.

9

Don't be frightened by the bowl in the draw, especially if you are a leader in a team. As a leader or even in singles, there will usually be plenty of room to draw the shot even if it is not right on the jack[10A].

Occasionally a bowl or bowls in your draw will force you to change your hand, but before you do, always try to get in a good second shot[10B-C].

10A

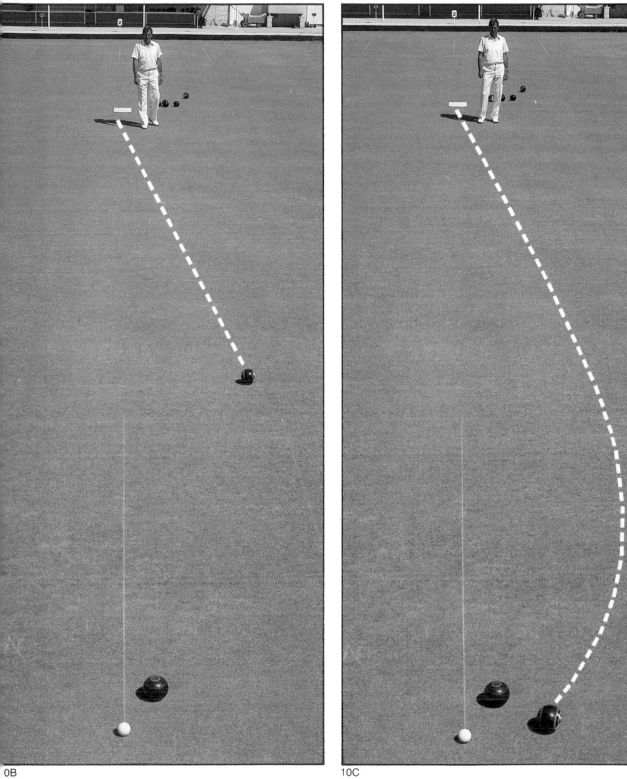

0B

10C

FAST GREENS

There has never been a true champion who is not adaptable. In reaching that goal of playing winning bowls, you will face all types of greens. You must conquer them all.

The best way in which to learn adaptability to any surface is in competition with a pennant side or in tournaments. At least half of your pennant matches will be away from home at clubs with all types of greens. The faster you learn to adapt your style and delivery on those greens, the faster you will reach your goals.

Fast greens allow the true artist to show his wares and touch. Such greens come in the warmer summer months when the surface is dry and hard and the grass is well cut. As I've mentioned before, these surfaces create little friction on a bowl's running surface, so that less propulsion is needed in delivery. On the mat, the bowl should be held well below waist level, thus reducing the amount of effort to be put into the delivery.

On fast greens, always attempt to draw slightly short and wide of the jack[11] because a minor loss of concentration will usually result in a long bowl. Going short and wide will compensate.

At the same time, a slight imperfection in delivery will almost certainly end in a bowl

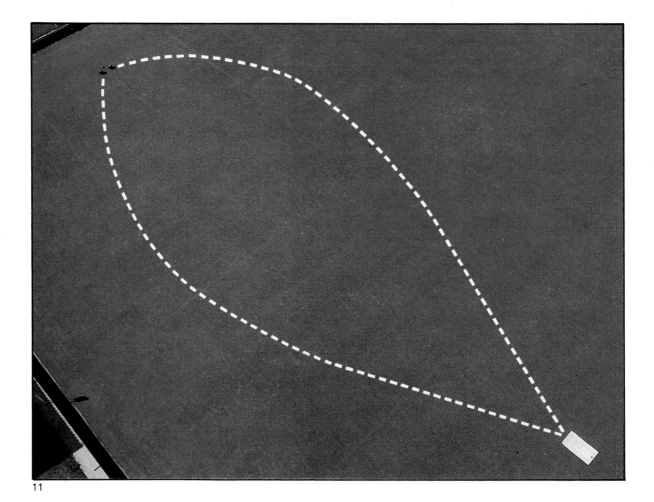

11

that is narrow and swinging across the head.

You need to be at your most alert and at your highest level of concentration on these surfaces. They are the most unforgiving of all greens.

SLOW GREENS

Spring and early summer are the times when greens can be at their slowest, especially in Australia's southern states. You can however, strike them at other times through the grass not being cut short, or damp through overwatering, rain or even a heavy dew.

In essence, a bowl must be delivered on a slow or heavy green[12] with greater momentum as it is inclined to sink lower in the grass.

On these types of greens, always go for the jack. Better still, attempt to trail it. On a 12 second green, I suggest a trail of about 30 centimetres (12 inches) and a further 30 centimetres for every half-second the pace of the green decreases.

If you miss the jack, then at least your bowls will finish behind the head where they certainly will be more useful.

Short bowls on these greens are little more than nuisances, and any lack of concentration will usually see yours becoming just that.

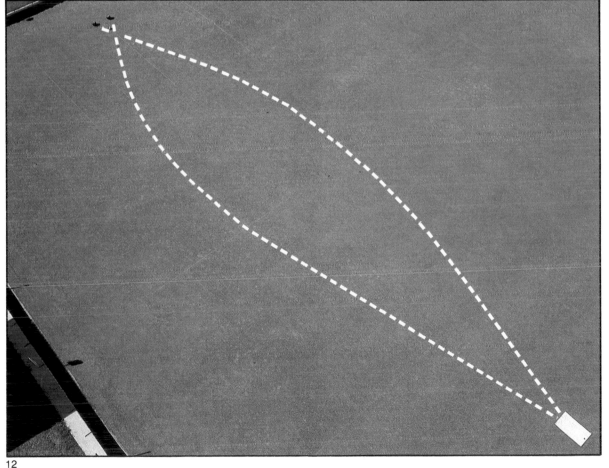

12

TOWARDS MASTERY

6

Good bowls is superb to watch and to play.

Finesse and precision are what this sport so amply offers — to both spectator and performer. Finesse is displayed in the art of draw-shot bowling; precision in the use of controlled shots — the yard-on, the running shot and the drive. Yet it must be remembered, the controlled shots are basically variations of the draw. With the draw, you may head towards mastery and the glories to be found in the game of lawn bowls. With controlled shots, you may well garner those glories.

At top level bowls, no man can expect to compete on level terms without the full armoury of shots. Let's look at them.

THE TRAIL OR TRUE YARD-ON

This can be one of the most intimidating shots you can play. Your opponents' expectation that you will trail the jack, can be almost as unnerving as the event itself. Either way, there's that extra bit of tension added to their game, a tension of which you can take advantage. To take the simplest of situations, your opponents may be holding shot; you have none, but you hold all the back bowls. The situation is ready-made for the jack to be shifted back so that it nestles among your bowls. Done successfully, the trail or yard-on can take you, for example, from one shot down to five up. It calls for finesse and accuracy — a shot to be played with confidence.

When attempting the trail, the idea is to visualise an imaginary jack in the position where you want your bowl to finish[1A]. On this head, I am a shot down but the situation calls for a trail of the jack back to my three bowls.

I can play it either hand, but have chosen the forehand because of a bad whip on the backhand[1B]. (Always be alert to green conditions and the way in which they can alter during a match.)

1A

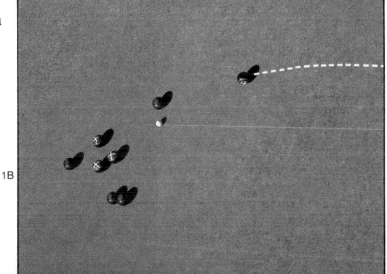

1B

1D

1C

To take the guess-work out of this demonstration, I've placed a second jack in the position visualised and am drawing to it[1C].

The result is clear — I'm four shots up after my last bowl[1D].

As I said, such a shot can be demoralising to an opponent, if played with accuracy — particularly early in the game. Think of it — your opposition is mildly comfortable in the belief that the end is his, but nervous in knowing that the situation is set up for your trail. You carry off the threat and suddenly, the opposition's confidence is shaken. At the same time, yours has been given a boost.

ATTACKING BOWLS
The Running Shot

If you can finesse an opponent into losing confidence with a trail, then how much more devastating the result with a similar shot played with pace.

This is the running shot, one to be played with equal accuracy but with possibly greater, though less predictable results. I've seen players with apparently winning hands, lose heart rapidly after one or two successful running shots. When your opponent realises that you are not only willing to have a go at running shots, but are also capable of delivering them with accuracy, any future head in the match is likely to be fraught with danger for him. In a sense, you will have established superiority.

Sometimes called the reaching shot, it is usually played with enough weight to carry to the ditch. But it doesn't really matter whether you are a metre or two over-weight, just so long as you hit the target.

Before delivery, select your aiming point on the bank (remember that it will be much narrower than for the draw) and assess the corresponding pace required for the shot.

Visualise as vividly as you can the perfect shot — the more vivid the picture in your mind, the more relaxed and confident you will feel.

On delivery, maintain your balance by trying not to put more effort than is necessary into the action and follow-through with that exaggerated movement of the arm, shoulder and body.

There are times when a running shot should be played and times when it should not. It depends on you and your mental make-up; on what type of player you are. Are you a gambler prepared to stake one shot on the chance of gaining more? Or are you satisfied with what you have?

2A

Here's an example of what I mean.

I am holding shot on this end, but it is early in the match and the situation opens the possibility of putting a dent in my opponent's confidence with a running shot[2A].

2B

2C

There are dangers of course, but in this set-up, my opponent's front bowls offer protection to my shot bowl[2B] and the worst result for me would be to go one down — hardly a great loss so early.

As always, I have assessed what I stand to gain or to lose. In fact the result is better than expected[2C]. The shot has taken the jack through to the ditch and I have gained an additional three shots. It was a calculated risk and one certainly worth taking.

3A

This is a case for a 'run through' shot[3A]. I am possibly four down but if I attempt to draw on the forehand, I could wreck on my own bowls and get nowhere.

The best answer to the problem is a running shot played on the backhand with enough weight to force my way through the opposition wall[3B]. Some players would try to promote their own bowls but that approach is risky at best.

The weight applied to my shot has run through that wall to reach jack high and take shot[3C] — a good result and an example of turning the tables when least expected.

There's a formula for the amount of weight or thrust required for a 'run through' shot. Basically, it is seven times the distance you wish to run after contact with the target bowl. In other words, if the opposition bowl is a metre short of the jack, you deliver your bowl to finish seven metres through.

If you merely want to turn the opponent's bowl out, the formula is three times the distance the bowl is to be moved.

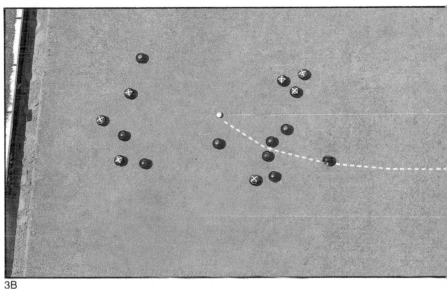

3B

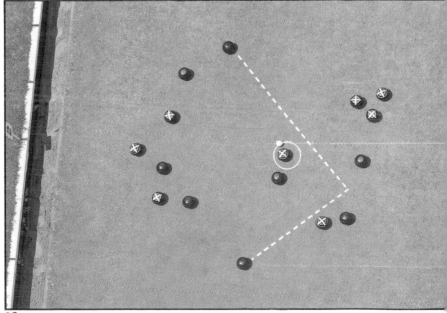

3C

The running shot is not easy to perfect, but even when it has been mastered, it should be used wisely, possibly even sparingly. An easy trap to fall into is over-use of this weapon, which becomes blunted, if your opponent gets too familiar with your pattern of play — and prepares accordingly. It is better that the running shot be used only when it has to be (as in the preceding photographs) and otherwise be reserved for its shock value.

One of the greatest difficulties top bowlers encounter is in playing the running shot on different grass surfaces. It is useful for you to know these differences before you find yourself in the same predicament.

In draw shot play, the difference between the bend bowls take on a tift dwarf surface and a green of bent grass is very little. However, because most tift dwarf greens are faster, a shot played at pace has very little time to bend. In other words, it is a straighter shot on tift dwarf.

Couch greens are entirely different. The finishing curve of the bowl is quite pronounced; the shoulder of the green (where your bowl visibly starts to turn) is further away from the mat than the shoulder of a tift dwarf or bent surface of similar pace. A bowl turns very little on couch until the last two or three metres of running.

So learn about your grasses and the effects they have on a bowl. One result of all this difference in grasses is that bowlers from the southern states tend to play their reaching shots too wide when they encounter the greens of the northern states.

ATTACKING BOWLS
The Drive

I'm often told that the drive is my trademark. Perhaps it is. If so, there are two reasons for it.

First, I have practised the drive more than most other bowlers and as a result, have become confident in its use. Second, I would not be able to get the results that I do without the basis of a sound, rhythmical draw-shot delivery. And that pleases me, because I know that I must be doing something right.

Show me a bowler with an unhurried, smooth drawing action with good body weight behind the delivery, and I'll show you someone with the potential to be a good driver. Yet there is one trap for such bowlers, albeit one that is easy to escape; I, myself, have fallen into it. While a lot of bowlers make the mistake of trying to drive too fast, I am usually the opposite and occasionally, I run into trouble by trying to guide the bowl. The results of both errors are immediately apparent.

The secret of the drive is in the action.

Let's start with the grip.

Basically it is the same grip as the one used in all other deliveries. Mine however, has one peculiarity, worked out and perfected through a great deal of practice and experiment.

Simply, I drive with the bowl tilted against the bias[4] which allows me to aim straight at the target. I tilt the bowl about one-quarter of a turn out towards the larger rings. What this does is to negate the bias and give me virtually a straight up-and-down line. Pace of the green and wind conditions govern the degree of tilt, but this is where all that practice, plus experience, teach you to assess just how much.

Next, let's consider the position of your feet on the mat.

For both forehand and backhand, the feet are placed on the left side of the centre line of the mat[5]. Left-handers stand on the right. Your feet must be pointing directly up the line you intend to drive and about three centimetres apart.

5

The stance is upright, but the knees relaxed and slightly bent, just as they would be for a draw shot[6].

6

The arm is held slightly out from the body to allow a smooth swing clear of the leg and hip.

The bowl is almost at eye-level[7] to enable a sighting to be taken over the running surface and onto the target, whether it's the jack or an opposition bowl.

Your mind is firmly fixed on the target, your grip on the bowl is firm, but relaxed.

Start your action 8^{A-H}, 9^{A-F}, stepping out long and straight, your arm going back, then forward in a long, fluent motion.

Finish with that deliberate follow-through towards the target. Most of all, keep to the fundamentals of the draw delivery, especially that smooth, rhythmical action.

Follow that drill and you will learn, as I did, that the drive is one of the most satisfying and spectacular shots in the game.

8A

8B

8E

8F

8C

8D

8G

8H

Something like eighty-five per cent of drives that miss, pass down the narrow side of the target. This indicates either a faulty delivery or a bad selection of the aiming point.

The latter is easily corrected.

If your problems stem from the former, I suggest that you try a longer step. It will help negate that tendency to 'pull' your hand and arm across your line of delivery.

Always drive as fast as you can, but within your capacity, and finish off with that long and deliberate follow-through. I cannot over-emphasise its importance.

9A

9B

9C

9D

9E

9F

To complete your locker of shots, you must be able to drive, with pace and accuracy. No bowler ever reaches the highest levels of the game without this shot. Those who make it to the top have practised long and hard. With experience, they have learned to choose the moment to drive. That moment is not always readily apparent.

This case[10A] is typical of a head you will often be confronted with. An initial study indicates a trail shot as a solution, with the only danger being the possibility of pushing one of my opponent's bowls onto the head.

10A

On this particular day however, a wind is gusting right to left across the green, and a trail may be risky. Up until now I have been driving confidently, so I decide to take out my opponent's nearest bowl[10B].

Three shots to me[10C] are further proof of the theory that if you are playing a particular shot really well on any day — make the most of it. If it happens to be the drive, use it to its fullest effect.

10B

10C

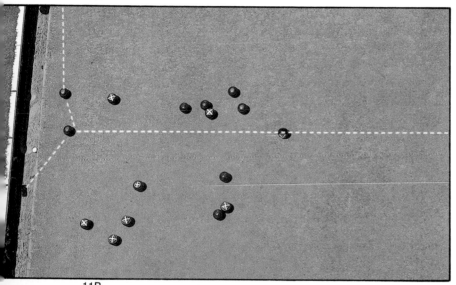

11A

11B

Bowls is not always curved and straight lines. It pays to know your angles, especially in a teams game with many bowls on the green.

In at least seven out of every ten matches, you'll strike this problem — the jack in the ditch. Sometimes, as in this case, there will be little hope of drawing the shot, but billiards players will see the solution at a glance.

The drive is the shot to play — straight at the opposition bowl nearest the jack[11A]. The one on its right, close to the ditch, is a toucher. Those two bowls are keeping me out of a fistful of shots and they have to go.

I play the drive so that it clips the left hand bowl on its right side[11B]. My bowl then cannons onto the toucher, sending it out of bounds.

Of course, my bowl has gone in at such a pace that it too, runs into the ditch[11c] — but with the opposition bowls cleared, I've gone from two down to five up.

11C

THE ANATOMY OF SINGLES

7

It is six o'clock in the evening of a hot summer's day in Melbourne.

The distant hum of traffic and the nearer roar of trains can be heard as city workers head home to begin a long weekend in the sun. On a suburban green two men in white, are seeking the singles championship of their club. Spectators are gathered around, but out on the green it is a very lonely place.

That's how it is in a singles match of any importance. For me, it is the loneliest place in the world at times, even though I have friends among those spectators on the bank; and more importantly, my parents and my wife, Ricky, are there to add their encouragement. In this case, it's certainly needed because I trail my opponent by many shots, by 17 to 5 in fact, and the immediate future looks dim. Worse, I have allowed outside circumstances to affect my game and my shots are going sour.

Then just when I need it most, comes a word from Ricky in the form of a prayer that is private between us. It is a steadier, the turning point. My concentration returns and with it, my shots. Inch by inch, I get back into the game and after three-and-a-half hours, the match and the title are mine by 31 shots to 30.

I can't help hearing the complimentary remarks from the bank. Clearly audible remarks like 'that's why he's a champion' and 'he never knows when he's beaten'. They're nice to hear and don't do my ego any harm, but deep down, I know what a close-run thing it has been and how I have almost handed the match to my opponent.

This story illustrates three things about the game of singles. You may have all the encouragement in the world, but ultimately you are on your own. No one can play the match for you or even tell you what to do. If you get into trouble there is only one person who can pull you out of it — you.

The second thing is that more than in any other type of game in bowls, singles demands total concentration on every bowl you put down. Many matches and titles have been lost when they should have been won, by players usually renowned for their concentration, who have lost their cool at vital moments.

Finally, the real excitement and attraction of a singles game lies not so much in the journey as in the arrival. Singles can produce surprise endings.

If I were going out today to play Rob Parrella in the final of a major singles tournament, I would make no forward plans. That may sound negative, but actually, it is the most positive approach one can take. Where there is only one opponent in a match, he can be full of surprises and you have to be alert and flexible to handle them. Where the match involves team play, some sort of tactical pattern can be worked out and often pays off.

Singles, on the other hand, can be quite different.

In playing Rob, I would marshall my psychological resources and attempt to concentrate for the entire match. I know Rob to be a skilfull and aggressive player, particularly on the drive. Should he be playing better than I, then I would deliberately set out to change the pattern of the game. I would become more aggressive myself, slowing down the overall pace and changing the length of the ends and the position of the mat.

The importance of the psychological approach to singles cannot be over-emphasised. Here's one example of what I mean[1A].

The scene is a singles match against Sid Meredith from Kenya, in the 1980 World Championships at Frankston. Down 15 to 19 in a match of 21 up, Sid was outdrawing me, so I decided to change tactics and attack.

When Sid drew his first shot six inches away and jack high, I drove[1B].

The shot was dead accurate, the end was killed and my opponent became so unsettled that I scored four, then two on the next two ends and won the match 21 to 19.

1A

1B

It is often said that singles is not a game for the gambler and I suppose to some extent, that is true. Yet if I hadn't gambled with that drive against Sid Meredith, I may not have gone on to win the silver medal at Frankston.

The secret is in knowing *when* to gamble. For the most part, it pays to play percentage bowls, since the singles game is mostly about drawing. I've known many bowlers who have tried to drive their way out of trouble, simply because they were being outdrawn. The usual result has been that they became drive-happy especially if the tactic worked a few times. In the end, the percentages catch up with such a player.

If you find yourself being constantly outdrawn, there is really only one way out of the problem. Get out on the practice green and develop your draw shots until they work. At the same time, take care not to swing to the other extreme and neglect to practise your controlled shots.

Consistency in drawing is another way of applying subtle psychological pressure on an opponent. If you can keep placing your shots on the head, time after time on any length, you not only gain the superior position, but also the upper hand by provoking acts of frustration in your opponent. He will lose concentration and make mistakes.

A match played in windy conditions can be the most challenging of all the tests you are likely to meet in your career. The toughest I can remember was the final match of the Frankston World Bowls. David Bryant and I found ourselves having to match shots and wits in a westerly of twenty knots, gusting to thirty at times. How we managed to display any sort of skill at all, I don't know. That day, I lost to David by two shots, but learned a great deal. One lesson was that it doesn't always pay to follow accepted theories about playing in wind.

Many top bowlers prefer long ends with the wind, and short ends against it.

I prefer the reverse because it makes me concentrate all the more. Indeed, the object is to out-concentrate my opponent, because in these condtions, a lapse can not only be costly in the short-term, it can also make it hard to recover lost ground.

Incidentally, when playing into the wind (anything 10 degrees either side of the jack) try to deliver generally off the outside edge of the mat, rather than the inside. This reduces the angle of draw to the jack and gives the wind less chance to work against the small or biassed side of the bowl.

In all singles matches, there is no easy or simple formula for success.

Each match has its own particular pattern and it has to be played as you see it. Only time and experience will teach you how to play winning singles, but if you adopt a positive mental attitude, acquire a smooth, rhythmical and accurate delivery and, above all, concentrate, then you will ultimately make it.

Remember to look for the opportunities in each end you play and when they come — as they always do — seize them with the best shot you can play. You may be pleasantly surprised with the end result. Like this one.

This is the last head of the Victorian Masters Final of 1968[2A] — one that I will long remember. I am leading 30 to 29 but two down on the head against Dr Leigh Fitzpatrick. The green is running at over 16 seconds and the jack has been trailed to the boundary line.

After walking to the head to check the position, and to give myself time to settle, I decided to draw the shot[2B]. For some inexplicable reason, I knew that I could draw the shot, impossible though it seemed to many people watching.

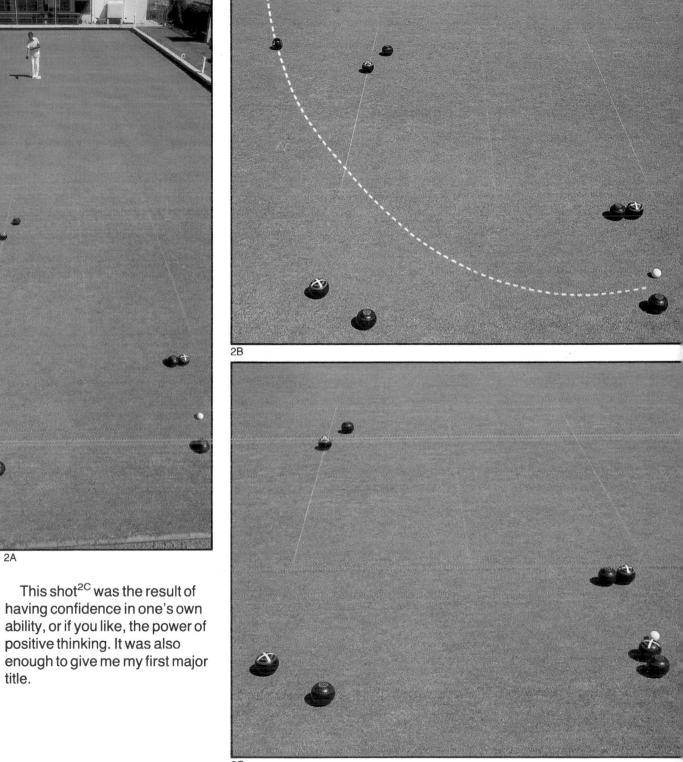

2A

2B

2C

This shot[2C] was the result of having confidence in one's own ability, or if you like, the power of positive thinking. It was also enough to give me my first major title.

3A

Or this one. I've re-created the set-up of the last head of the final in the World Open Singles played at Christchurch in New Zealand[3A]. The finalists are Peter Belliss, of New Zealand, and Barry Salter, from Newcastle, New South Wales. Peter's bowls carry the crosses. In a 25-up match, Barry leads 23 shots to 22 and on this head, holds three more. The green is running about 14 seconds and there is a gusty, fish-tailing wind.

Barry's shot bowl is a toucher. Remember that he holds second and third and his position appears to be impregnable. The backhand is almost completely blocked and because of the wind, the forehand is almost unplayable — almost, but not quite.

In desperation, Belliss decides to drive on the forehand[3B] in an attempt to save the game in any way he can. It is his last bowl.

To everyone's amazement, including Belliss', the drive takes out Salter's three shots[3C], leaving the Newcastle man with only one very short bowl on the green, and Belliss with three shots for the match and the title.

If ever proof was needed that a match is not over until the last bowl is down, then this was it. It's worth remembering Belliss' last, desperate drive the next time you are down, but not quite out.

3B

The other side of the coin is in thinking the match is yours when you are holding a handy lead and are only one or two shots from home. That is the time to do your damnedest. I've seen too many players falter at the last hurdle, simply because they had convinced themselves that they had already won. I'm not suggesting for one moment that this was the case with Barry Salter. Far from it. He had fought hard and long and was in a superb situation on the last end, only to see Peter Belliss get up in the last stride with that most amazing of shots.

3C

I'm often asked at what pace a bowl should be played. The answer, naturally, depends on the situation at the head. But instinctive judgment based on experience, will guide you in determining the weight of a delivery[4A]. It should also be remembered that you will almost certainly be faced with at least two choices of shots in any situation. Making the correct choice is what winning bowls is all about.

4A

4B

Faced with this situation[4B], I would choose to play with something more than draw-weight.

In fact, I am attempting to play the shot to finish about four metres past the jack.

The factors in this decision are:

1 The shot bowl may be moved far enough so that my three 'seconds' would count[4C].

2 If I am narrow, and contact my short bowl, then there still would be sufficient pace to remove my opponent's shot bowl.

3 If I am narrower still, I can run through the opposition's short bowl and into the head.

As things turn out[4D], my bowl has scored a direct hit on the shot bowl, taken it out and left me three shots up. In this type of situation, it's wise to play from the outside edge of the mat to provide a greater margin.

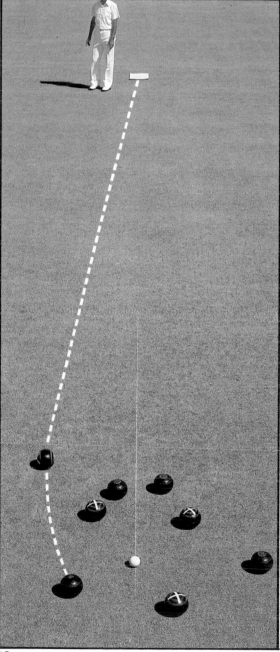

4C

4D

Drawing close to the jack is the heart of the single-handed game.

The old-timers will tell you that a good draw-shot bowler will beat a good driver every time. It's a bit like the big-man, little-man theory in boxing, but things don't always turn out that way.

A good singles player has mastery over all types of shots, but this takes time and much practice. If you come up against an opponent who is willing to drive without compunction, remember your priorities. Draw into the jack with your first two bowls, then go for position behind the head if he disturbs it. With your last shot on any end, whether you are up or down, play it as if your life depends on it.

There is the other side to singles which we will talk about in a later chapter. I've called it 'the inner game' for fairly obvious reasons.

For now, remember that no champion ever got to be one without practice: first the draw, then the controlled shots, finally the drive. Above all, remember that the chief demand of singles is for concentration of the highest order.

Take all that in, and you won't go far wrong.

TEAMING UP

8

If singles play demands skill, wits and concentration, then teams play calls for all that — and more. As the title implies, there must be team-work whether the game is pairs, triples or fours.

In Australia, most bowls is played in teams, either in pennant, interstate competition, or just a friendly roll-up after work has ended for the day. Whatever the size of a club, it usually has only just enough rinks available to cater for its members. So it makes sense to get as many players onto the green at a time, as possible.

By playing as a team member, the newcomer learns more quickly what bowls is all about. There is another benefit, too. Once he is on the green, a man who only minutes before, may have been weighed down with the cares of the world, will quickly forget them. He will be among friends.

Let us deal with each team game separately, for each provides its own style of play, approach and even psychology.

PAIRS

'Partners' perhaps is a better name for this game. It involves patience, tolerance, mutual support and plenty of imagination. Pairs play gives me almost as much satisfaction as singles — to be able to think and work with another as one, is a splendid feeling.

Pairs should be played like a game of fours with one man playing lead and third and the other playing second and skip. In Australia we play pairs differently from say, the British and the South Africans, who operate under the international rule of each man playing his four bowls in succession. I believe ours is a better game because it provides greater scope for each shot, and allows more flexible tactics. Here, each man plays his four bowls in units of two alternately. This method means a match may take longer, with the constant changing of ends, and may eventually end under growing pressure from many quarters.

As I said, the nature of pairs means that it is an extremely tactical game, and since each player has four bowls, you will find it to be of a higher standard. The jack will be moved more often than in a fours match, so it is essential to keep the number of short bowls to a minimum. Never worry if you are playing lead and your first two bowls are through the head. It is better to err on the long side since back bowls can be extremely valuable in pairs with the jack moving around such a lot.

The idea is to get two or at the most, three good bowls on the head, then look for position. Remember that, like chess, pairs is essentially a positional battle, and that greed is often punished.

1A

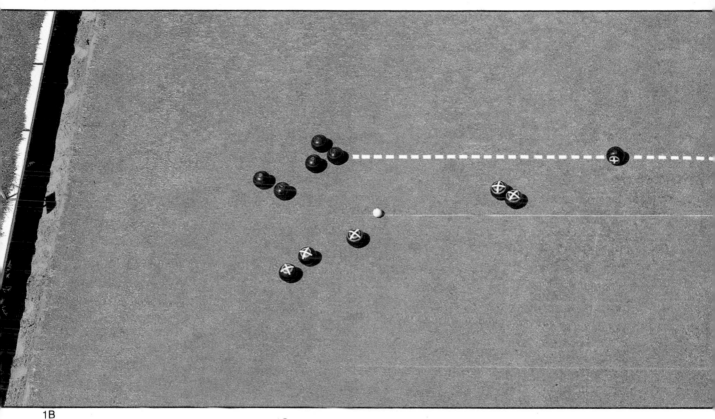

1B

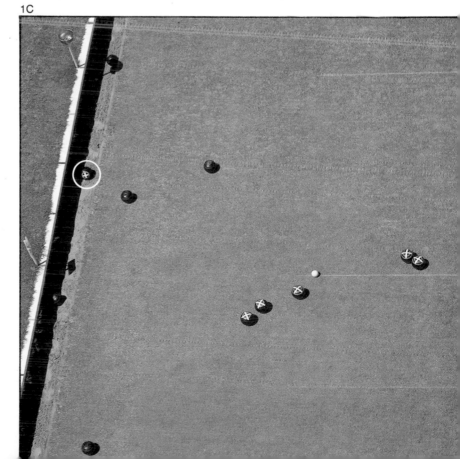

1C

Here's a good example of what I mean[1A].

For identification, my partner's and my bowls carry crosses. The head holds great danger for us, as an opposition trail shot could well leave us five or six shots down.

I choose to drive at the opposition's bowls, removing the danger and improving our own position[1B].

A direct hit with the drive on the forehand has cleared all the offending bowls and left me holding five shots[1C].

2A

2B

A lead must avoid creating too big a target through placing all his bowls into the head. It may be marvellous drawing but a good opposition skipper will soon destroy the head with either a drive or a running shot, or at the least, a trail. You can find a disaster on your hands very smartly by ignoring the danger of an opposition with the controlled shot as their stock-in trade.

At the same time, courage and coolness and an analytical mind can often pay off, particularly when your opponents least expect it — and this can be demoralising for them.

In this type of situation[2A], always think before you act. Ask yourself: what can I gain, and what can I lose? I'm two shots down and the obvious shot, at first glance, is to drive at those two opposition bowls. But is it?

This is my shot[2B] — a draw on the forehand with little risk and even a possibility of trailing the jack to my own bowls, thus going from two down to two up.

Now let's go back to the head as it was[2C] and look at the position before I came to the mat. Those two opposition shot bowls certainly are a tempting target for a drive.

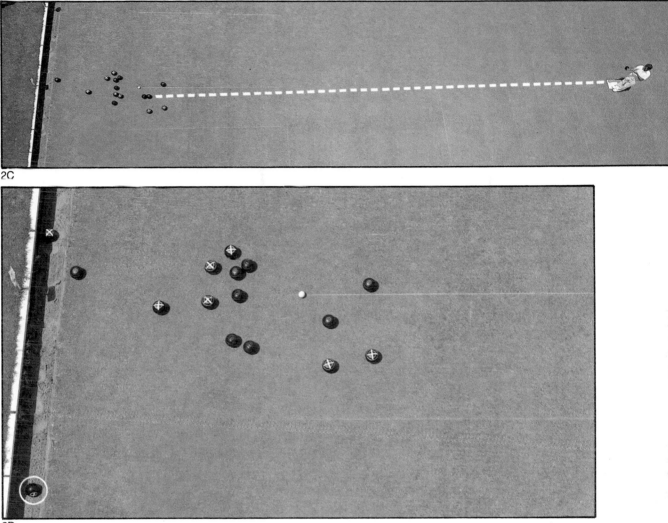

2C

2D

If I drive here's the probable result[2D]. The two shot bowls form a 'plant', as they say in billiards, and with my drive, I've pushed them onto my nearest bowls, knocking them well out of the head and leaving me a possible five shots down.

Successful bowls is percentage bowls, and in pairs prudence often wins out over pile-driving.

Most top bowlers agree that the simplest trap a pairs skipper can fall into, is the habit of not concentrating enough with his first two shots. It is his job to consolidate by drawing if he is down in numbers of shots, or look for position if his partner has done his job and drawn two good shots.

As much as straight-out ability, the pairs game revolves around position, courage, brains and imagination. Each partner, since he is playing in two positions, must possess all the shots. Each has to know what the other is thinking and trying to do.

In a nutshell, pairs partners run in double harness. Good ones go together like bacon and eggs.

TRIPLES

I have to be candid and admit that triples is no great favourite of mine.

I know it is a form of bowls popular in many parts of Australia and is the basis for many tournaments staged at club level on social occasions. At higher levels, such as at the World Championships, triples can be keenly competitive.

However, to me it is too much of a skipper's game and as a team involvement form of play, it does not have the attraction of pairs. The tactics of triples are much the same as those of pairs, even though each player delivers three bowls. The lead's main task is to draw his three bowls as close to the jack as he can. The middle man, who should be capable of playing all shots well, then has the task of converting or saving.

The skipper really controls the play and should be planning to gain position sooner than in a fours game because with three bowls per man, there is a good chance that the jack will be moved quite often. It means also that the skip has to be able to play the pressure shot to save, because with three bowls, an opposition skip is unlikely to fail altogether.

FOURS

For as long as bowls is played, there will be arguments about who is the most important player in a game of fours.

Some have it that the skipper is the most vital, since it is he who controls the tactics and thus, the game. Others put forward the case for third; the second has his supporters as does the lead who, it is claimed, provides the basis for victory or defeat.

Over the years I've heard them all, and I must say that I am not impressed. There is only one element for success in a fours game, and that is for each member of the team to do his part and blend with his mates into a solid combination. Often I've seen four fairly ordinary bowlers defeat four above-average players, simply because they harmonised, communicated and played as a team. The others failed because they didn't — perhaps because they were temperamentally unsuited to each other, or because they were, at heart, individualists.

Fours is a team game and yet each member has a different job to do.

Leader

- The leader sets the pattern of play and virtually decides whether the team plays attacking or defending bowls. He does this by the length to which he rolls the jack and whether or not he gets his two bowls close to the jack. Those are the leader's two main tasks.
- If you are playing lead, you should aim to get shot, but if you don't, then it is necessary for you to get at least one bowl near to the jack. It gives your team-mates something to work on.
- Never 'niggle' at the head unless the skipper asks you to — and that's not likely.
- Try and play one side of the green — forehand one way and backhand the other. Once you've settled on the hands to play, stay with them unless your team is being beaten or your skipper recommends that you change.
- Maintain your concentration, particularly on your own match and do everything you can to encourage your team-mates.

Second

To play second in a team of four demands all-round versatility. It is the second's task to counter his lead's failure to get shots close to the jack or convert when the opposition lead has gained an advantage.

That type of role calls for a second who can draw, wrest out opposition shots or break up a head. At the higher level of competition, it is essential for the second to be a good driver. That's why the players selected in state or national teams tend to be specialists in their positions.

If you are chosen to play second, be certain about what you are asked to do by the skipper. Be ready, but don't get onto the mat until you are certain. Above all, a second must have confidence in his skipper who will often call for him to play shots which from the mat, often look to be Impossible.

I've found that the biggest temptation for a second is to attempt to 'reach' an opposition bowl lying jack high when the skipper has called for a draw. The skip, from his end, knows it is vital to have one on the head but it won't happen if you are tempted to niggle at that jack high bowl and miss altogether. It can be a tough life playing second, but even tougher for a skipper if his second doesn't do what is asked of him.

The other jobs for a second in a rink are mainly housekeeping — keeping the scorecard and the scoreboard on the bank, but don't forget you have to be precise about these, too. Getting the scores wrong or mixed can be, at the least, an embarrassment. Often it's much more; it could end in the entire team losing points.

Third

Probably the best way to describe the third's role is to call him the foreman on the job.

Basically, his qualities must be those of a sound, all-round second, plus plenty of experience. The latter is essential, because he has to be able to read a head and advise the skipper at the other end when asked to do so. Experience will have taught the third

to be cool in a crisis. Often he will be called on to play a crucial shot when the team is in trouble. The third can be worth his salt for a mere half-a-dozen 'big' shots during a match, because those shots could mean the difference between a win and a loss.

Some other tips for a third:

- Be decisive when asked a question by your skip.
- Develop the judgment to decide who is holding shot.
- Be exact, steady and confident when measuring for shot.
- If you see the possibility of a big score and the skipper hasn't, call him to the head and explain.
- Never put doubts into the skipper's mind. His job is hard enough as it Is.

Skipper

This man is like any other captain in any other team sport.

The job demands that he be experienced, understanding, calm, a good tactician, a good psychologist, and it helps if he is a good bowler.

Over the years, thousands upon thousands of words have been written and spoken about the essentials of being a skipper. I've watched the good ones and learned much. I have stored that knowledge and used it when my chance has come.

In summary:

A good skipper must be positive and decisive, have a sense of humour, and command of all shots. He must also be confident and alert to changes in conditions.

At the end of it all, comes the hard part. If the team is beaten, the skipper invariably has to carry the blame — that is where it will be sheeted home. If the team wins, everybody wins, not just the skipper.

The responsibility for the team's approach and tactics is the skipper's, but he cannot carry them out alone. His major task, therefore, is to instil in the other three players the fact that they are playing with him and not as individuals, although each has to carry out his allotted task.

If a skipper can make his team a happy one, then half the battle has been won. That is why I am always aware of the need to be pleasant and tactful — not condemning a struggling player, but encouraging him. I try to avoid too many gestures, because they can be misunderstood at the other end of the green, as can too many comments.

Experience teaches a skipper what type of tactics to adopt in each match, but as a general rule fours in many ways is like pairs. With so many bowls delivered during an end, the jack is bound to be moved around. Therefore, never leave your back position unprotected. Count on your opposite number playing the perfect shot, rather than failing. That way, you won't be caught unawares or become careless.

Ultimately, no matter how good a skipper is in all other departments of the game, his reputaton is based on the results he achieves. So if the score on the board is what counts in the end, a skipper always looks for the shot that will get his team out of trouble or the one that will add to the score.

That is one secret of winning team bowls.

Here are some more.

When things look blackest, there's usually at least one way to tip the odds in your favour. In this case[3A], it is almost impossible to drive or run the shot bowl out direct. The jack is in the ditch.

The way out is to play a running shot onto my bowl[3B] (carrying cross and touching the shot). In snooker, it's called a 'plant' or a 'set'. In bowls in Queensland, it's called a 'charlie' — I don't know why.

The method works, anyway. Here[3C], my running shot has pushed out the opposition bowl (not a toucher) and left me five shots up.

3A

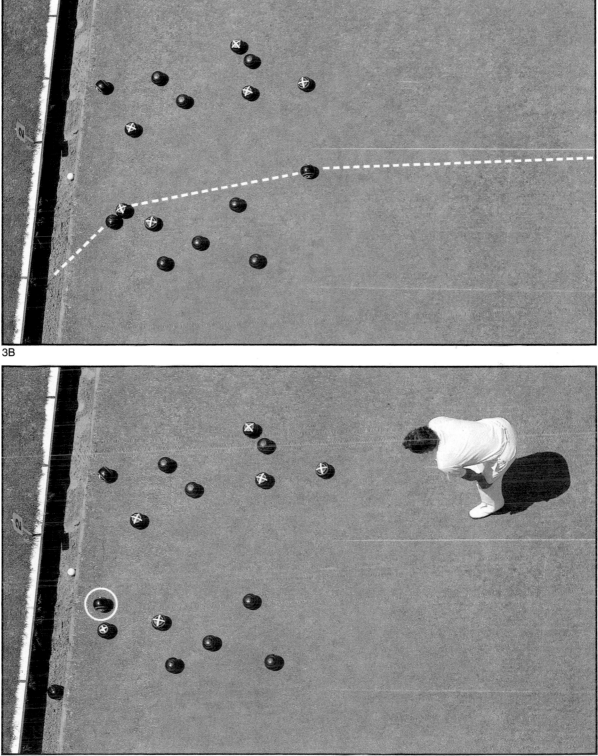

3B

3C

Here's[4A] another 'plant'. This type of head is not always obvious and the inexperienced player might opt for a draw, although the odds would be against him succeeding.

'The plant' is lined up with the opposition shot bowl[4B], and my running shot really is a no-risk play. In making my decision, I considered I had more to gain than lose.

The result[4C] is that not only has my previous bowl been promoted to shot, the bowl I have just delivered has stopped in the count and the opposition bowl, previously shot is well out. Four shots up is a big dividend.

4A

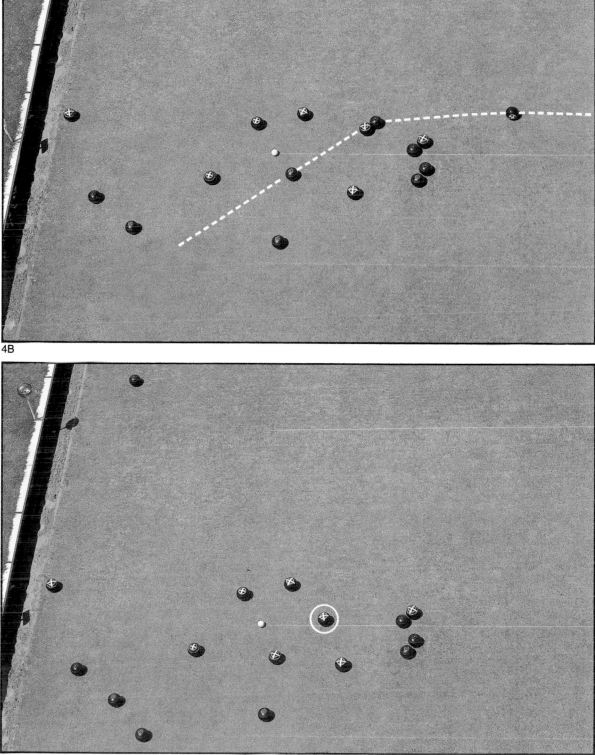

4B

4C

5A

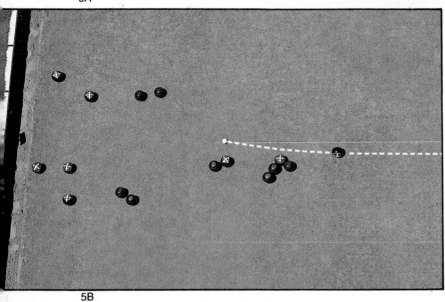

5B

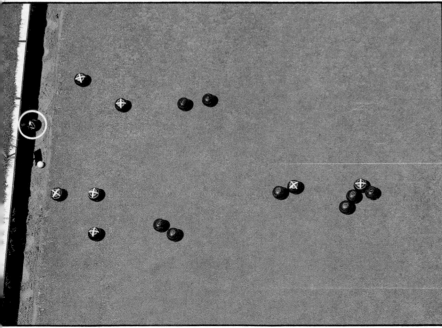

5C

Bowls is all about seizing opportunities and this one[5A] is a chance to pick up some 'runs'.

Even though I'm holding shot, the position is a precarious one and the opportunity lies in those five back bowls of mine. There is some risk involved as it is possible to 'nick' the jack and go three down. Yet, it remains a percentage play rather than a gamble.

I play the shot[5B] at almost drive pace, but on the backhand to give my shot bowl some protection. The aim is to take the jack back.

That is where the jack ended[5C], being struck full-face. It's the type of shot to be played early in a match in an attempt to demoralise the opposition.

6A

There's nothing in bowls quite so exciting as the drive. It is also a potent weapon, that gives both satisfaction and rewards. Here[6A] I am two shots down and the target is an obvious one.

Always drive with your bowl swinging away from danger, as in this instance[6B]. In driving at the two shot bowls, there is little risk. In fact, should I hit either side of the left-hand bowl there is a strong possibility both bowls will go.

The result[6C] is exactly that and I am two shots up. That, surely, is satisfaction.

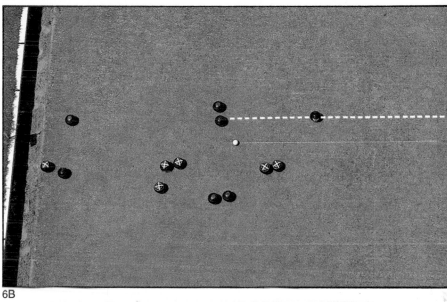

6B

6C

THE INNER GAME

9

Bowls has always suffered from the slings and arrows of the uninitiated.

Without having first tried it, they sneer at a game that is too slow, not physical enough and which calls for no great thought. It must be that way they reason, otherwise how can it be played by old people?

How little they know!

Since one can play bowls over longer periods and for more years than most other sports, it can be more demanding, both mentally and physically. The average player is on the green at least four days of every week in the season. If he wishes, he can travel and play somewhere seven days a week all year round.

Don't delude yourself that you don't have to be fit to do that. Take the case of a bowler playing in a tournament of, say three matches of fifteen to twenty ends in a day. He is out there for seven or eight hours, walks up to eight to ten kilometres and bends and delivers more than half a ton of bowls. This is not an exaggeration; it is what competitors at the World Championships did at Frankston in 1980 every day for eighteen days. Knowing what lay ahead of me in that event, I trained for months beforehand, walking and jogging up to ten kilometres every day. The world titles experience cannot be considered to be average but in the higher levels of the sport it can happen. The rigours of tournament play are such that you need to be very fit to maintain the necessary physical and mental effort.

Yet I rate the physical side of bowls at only thirty per cent of the game. Most of the action cannot be seen, only guessed at. It takes place inside the head, which is why I place great emphasis on what I like to call the 'inner game'. This is the psychology of bowls, the thinking man's approach to your own game and to that of your opponent. It is what the uninitiated do not see and therefore do not understand.

EXPERIENCE

Playing the inner game is the key to winning bowls, but it cannot be learned overnight. That undisputed champion, Glyn Bosisto, once said that it took six years to become a good bowler and another six to become a champion. I don't doubt for a moment that 'Bossie's' yardstick was true in his heyday. In the 'eighties, however, the correct physical and mental approach can cut this time-scale to four and four. The essential ingredient is experience and if you can get it while you are young and fit, then you have a head start. Seize every opportunity to get experience, be it in pennant competition, club events or the tournaments which seem to take place every week somewhere in your city, town or state.

Coming into the game when I did, I was able to pick up experience by taking part in the top-class invitation events which started around that time. In these, I was able to play against only top bowlers. Of course, you have to be on the way to being one yourself for these events, but that is all part of the challenge and you never stop learning. To underline the point, I received my first invitation to one of these tournaments in 1965, five years after starting out in the game and the year in which I won my first club championship. There's no doubt it was a turnaround year for me. Only three years later, at the age of thirty-three, the experience gained helped take me to my first major win — the Victorian Masters Singles title after only eight years in bowls.

Acquiring, retaining and applying the lessons are very much part of the inner game. You must learn to decide which shot to play and equally important, the correct method of playing that particular shot.

One quick way to gain experience is to play regularly against different opponents for side bets. It sounds drastic but the method has the advantage, or disadvantage if you like, of learning to play and win under pressure — or go broke.

TEMPERAMENT

While all this is going on, you will be quietly picking up and developing the mental toughness so vital in any sportsman who wants to get to the top and stay there. To ensure the process you must practise, again and again. Experience combined with constant, intelligent practice teaches you many things, not the least of them being the cultivation of confidence in your own ability. That is my definition of temperament.

In short, the more you play and the more you practise, the more confident you will become. Your victories will become more numerous, your failings fewer. With confidence comes the ability to think positively about what you are doing; enabling you to push out those mind-gnawing doubts. The mind becomes relaxed and so too does the body.

Lack of doubt has other benefits. You are alert to changing conditions during a match, to your opponent's weaknesses, or faults that can creep into your own game. Remember that one of the essentials of bowls is the ability to correct your own faults during a match. If for example, your first bowl is short, then you have to correct with your next. To do that you must know what was wrong with the first bowl. It is here that the alert mind comes into its own.

As I've said before Glyn Bosisto is without doubt the best bowler Australia has ever produced. At his peak, the factor that made him stand taller than anyone else was his ability to concentrate. His concentration was always better than that of his opponent: he could shut his mind to distractions around the green and focus on the task of winning.

This approach did not always win him great popularity with casual spectators, but that is understandable as they did not comprehend his dedication and will to win. Too many Australians seem to have this unfortunate trait of looking for opportunities to 'knock' their sporting champions.

Glyn's concentration was at its highest level when he faced the prospect of defeat, which was seldom enough. To paraphrase Dr Johnson, Glyn Bosisto was a subscriber to the view that nothing concentrates the mind so wonderfully as the threat of defeat. Dr Johnson used the word 'hanging', not defeat, but in Glyn's case, they probably meant much the same. Like all champions, he hated to lose — he still does, for that matter.

Speaking of champions, David Bryant holds the theory that there is no such word as defeat — it must never be thought, let alone spoken — only the word, victory. That theory and the Bosisto story serve only to emphasise the point about confidence, concentration and temperament. One sure way to achieve concentration on the green is this.

Before your shot, particularly a vital one, visualise yourself playing the perfect bowl — draw, drive or controlled shot — whatever is called for. Imagine it as vividly as you can, then step onto the mat, automatically recalling all the points about feet placement, grip and stance, etcetera. The chances are that you *will* play the perfect shot.

To take it one step further with a specific example: you are shots down, the bowl in hand is your last and you have to draw to win the end. Visualise yourself drawing to a bare jack with no other bowl on the green. Forget they are there, or you will create doubt in your mind. You will not be thinking positively.

After the World Championships at Frankston, I struck up a friendship with a man named Jim Goulding. Jim is a clinical hypnotherapist who has helped many sportsmen and sporting teams to reach great heights. When we met, I was in a bit of a trough, coming mid-way through a long, hard season. The main problems were too much bowls and a build-up of pressure within. On top of this, there had been a rapid growth in my responsibilities and work as a bank manager. The result was a spate of minor health problems and a drop in my performance on the green during the 1980-1981 season. While Jim was teaching me the art of relaxation, he was also working on the theory that during my matches, I was spending far too much time analysing my bad shots and thus building up a negative mental attitude. He was right, and his teachings worked, enabling me to restore confidence in myself and find good form again. One of my biggest remaining problems, and perhaps it is yours too, is becoming so wrapped up in the emotional side of a game that it interferes with my concentration. It is a trap I must be alert to in each match I play.

PRACTICE

Preparation for any match does not start just a day or two beforehand.

It must go back a long, long way, perhaps to the beginning of the season or even the previous year. How you practised over those months could determine how you will play in the match.

Basically, intelligent practice means the cultivation of a 'perfect' delivery, one that is well-grooved and will stand the rigours and the pressures of any match. You will recall my earlier statement that the draw is the basic shot in bowls; all the rest are merely variations or extensions of the draw. It follows then that a large part of your practice time should be spent on perfecting the draw; or to put it another way, perfecting your delivery.

A summary of my practice methods indicates the following breakdown:

Draw-shot bowling — 95%
Trail or controlled shots — 3%
Drives — 2%

That's how your time should be spent, too.

If there are faults in your delivery, you should practise that shot or hand until they are eradicated.

If you are having problems with a particular length, then work hard at strengthening that weakness. This approach has paid off for me. For example, in 1965, at the Ararat Club in Victoria, one of the weaknesses in my game was playing long ends. So at every opportunity I practised 'ditch to ditch' in an endeavour to iron out the fault. Without all that effort I would not have won my first club championship that year. My opponent in the final was a renowned long-end player, but after the weeks of practice at that length I was able to match him.

Do not however, concentrate for too long on one aspect of your game. Match those figures above and you will strike a fair balance in overall practice.

MATCH PREPARATION

Before any match, the top bowlers should always prepare themselves mentally, especially if the match is an important one. Each will have his own method. I've worked out mine over the years to the point where it is routine, yet simple and effective. Oddly enough, it was only recently that I discovered Sir Robert Menzies followed almost exactly the same method before he gave any political or after-dinner speech. It seemed to work well for him, too.

By all means, do some thinking about the forthcoming match during the lead-up days, but on the night before, forget all about it. That is the time for relaxing, preferably with a good book, but definitely not one about bowls. The second furthest thought from your mind should be bowls; the last thing should be the match itself. If you do find thoughts about the match stealing into your mind, let them come. They won't stay long if you don't attempt to fight them. You will relax and have a good night's sleep.

The next day (the morning of the match) you'll be easy in your mind and raring to go. Plan to arrive at the club half-an-hour before the match is due to start. Those thirty minutes will be the most critical of all in preparing your mind. If possible, go for a brisk walk or do some muscle-loosening exercises. They will help you to overcome that pre-match tightness that all good players experience.

Then get away by yourself for from five to ten minutes. Sit in the car or in a quiet corner of the locker room by yourself, breath deeply and gather your thoughts. One way to do this is to concentrate on something, a small object such as a keyhole or a mark on the wall. Examine it in all its aspects: shape, colour, size, length, breadth, any peculiarities, so that your mind is focused on something specific and not flitting from one thing to another.

Do that for a minute or two and you will find that gradually you are transferring your thought processes to the manner in which you are going to tackle the match and your opponent. In your mind you will see yourself on the mat, going through your delivery and follow-through, smoothly and with rhythm.

It is time to meet your opponent.

THE VITAL FACTOR

Now, we come to the heart of the inner game — on the green.

It seems to be the fashion nowadays to deride the concept of winning.

These 'knockers', I believe, have their values confused. Certainly some aspects of some sports, as well as some sportsmen, have earned a tarnished image, so that those who play by the rules, literally as well as in spirit, stand out like candles in the darkness.

The fact remains that ours is a competitive world, no matter how much some wish it were not so, and competition is the root of all sport. There has to be a winner and a loser. Which would you rather be? It is a question that must be faced honestly. To win you have to beat an opponent, and to beat him you must *want* to beat him.

Your practice and mental preparations have given you the confidence in your own ability. From the beginning of the match, you must wear this air of confidence so that it can be seen and felt by your opponent.

While I certainly deplore gamesmanship, there must be an element of psychological warfare in any match. It begins even before a bowl is delivered. If I win the toss and the mat, I usually throw a medium-length end and continue on that length until my opponent wins the mat. If true to form, he will then reveal his strength by rolling the jack to his favourite length. When this happens and I win the mat back, I will always return to 'his' length. In this way, you can gain a psychological advantage by displaying your own confidence in your ability to beat him at his own game. He has nowhere to go and even if he does prove too strong on his favourite length, you can always reverse the situation when you eventually win an end.

During the game there is a need for a constant re-appraisal of the situation. It may seem unimportant if you are playing well and winning, but any change in the game can threaten your control and you have to be alert and responsive to these psychological moments. If on the other hand, you strike a lean period, a re-appraisal of your delivery, tactics and mental approach can be enough to get you going again.

First, have a good think about your delivery and follow-through. If you need time to do it, walk up to examine the head, even if you know what the situation is there. Your rhythm and follow-through must be working properly to maintain consistent line and length. If they are not, and the results are obvious, then take your time and get back to basics with your next shot.

Second, give the situation a re-appraisal. Your concentration can be affected in several ways — by engaging in conversation with your opponent or spectators, or by watching every single delivery put down by your opponent. Fill in time between your shots by looking about at the scenery, or perhaps the sky, for there are few things more restful. Take care though, not to waste time and keep your opponent waiting. If you are distracted just as you are about to bowl, leave the mat and return when you are ready once more. If allowed, as in international rules, follow your bowl to the head from time to time. It helps to reduce tension.

When you find yourself being beaten constantly on the draw-shot, don't hesitate to change the pace of the game. Only in the extreme should you speed it up. Preferably, slow the game down and when you have the mat, change the length or the area of the green being used. It helps to break up your opponent's rhythm. I recall playing the redoubtable John Dobbie in the Victorian Masters a few years ago. To me, John plays at an appallingly fast pace and after I had led 16-1, I found myself down 17-18. My mistake was in trying to match John's pace. I was playing him at his own game, in other words. After a re-appraisal, I consciously set out to slow things down. There were plenty of anxious moments after that, but the change in tactics worked in the final result. Incidentally, both John and his brother David have that confident, superior air about them

which tends to make their opponents doubtful about their chances.

When the going gets tough in a match, keep cool particularly in these last few ends when the score is close. Take your time and again, walk slowly to the head to give yourself a few moments' break. It ensures that you don't deliver the bowl before you have had time to think about it. Picture for a moment all those great sportsmen you have seen over the years. Many take their time before committing themselves to an action.

Gary Player, the South African golfer, is a good example. I saw him once, during the tense moments of the final round of a tournament, bend down and pick up a blade of grass. There was nothing casual about the movement, although it may have looked that way to some. What Player was doing in fact, was giving himself time to breathe deeply and slowly which is a recognised way of easing tension. He went on to win.

The blending of experience, practice, confidence, concentration, preparedness and determination can be seen in any of the really top bowlers. You know them by their victories and the way in which they achieve them. You know them too, by the way they handle the rewards of those victories — it is far harder to be a winner than a loser. Less is expected of a loser.

Then there are the plain good bowlers. I have seen many play superb bowls to win a tough match, then in the next round, play poorly to lose against a man they should have beaten. They go on doing this all their bowling lives, never learning the secrets of application to the job in hand.

There is only one match that counts. The one you are playing.

There is only one bowl that counts. The one in your hand. Play it like the champions do — as if it were your last.

When you do that, you are ready to play winning bowls.

THE CHAMPIONS

10

If results are what really count, then the line between success and failure is very fine. There is no one who is so good that he will win every time. It is too much to ask of any mortal.

The trick of a champion is to win more often than lose and to have the ordinary sense to realise that he can do no more than that.

I would like to tell you about sixteen champions. Over the past fifteen years, I have known and played with, and against, them all. Each has given me many pleasurable and memorable moments. Each possesses and exemplifies particular qualities that make them champions. If one were able to extract those qualities and to build a composite from them, the result would be the ultimate winning bowler: the compleat champion.

GLYN BOSISTO   His ability to concentrate is the outstanding factor that set Glyn apart from all other bowlers in Australia from the late 1940s through to the mid-'sixties. There is no doubt that he possessed other great qualities but to me, his concentration was the most outstanding one.

DAVID BRYANT   A study of the greats in all types of sport over a long period leads me to the conclusion that with the possible exception of Swedish tennis star Bjorn Borg, this Englishman has the best temperament of all. David exercises outstanding control over his emotions and has the ability to switch in seconds, from complete relaxation to full concentration. It is a rare ability.

DENNIS DALTON   His delivery must be rated amongst the smoothest in the world and is particularly suited to the slower surfaces in Victoria. Yet, he has not had such success on faster greens, possibly due to his free action, and lack of opportunities to play more frequently in the North.

BOB KING   A prolific winner of singles events, Bob is to me, an enigma in the game of lawn bowls. His quietness, combined with an apparent lack of enthusiasm, belies the reality of Bob King as a deep-thinker who possesses enormous amounts of self-confidence. Like many top sportsmen, he suffers at times, from a build-up of pressure over a long season, resulting in a loss of form. While Bob has a rather nervous disposition, one would never think it to see him deliver a bowl. His delivery is the most rhythmical I've seen and he adapts easily to all types of greens, although he admits to a dislike for the slower ones.

JOHN DOBBIE   A colourful player in his heyday and the possessor of a powerful drive. To emphasise what I said earlier, John's paramount ability has been the way he has exerted influence over his opponents. By displaying a superior air, well-founded or not, he has quite often destroyed the confidence of his opposition.

GORDON LANGDON As great a fighter and draw shot player as I've seen, I don't think Gordon ever knew the meaning of defeat. If I were eight shots down and had to choose one man to draw me out of trouble, that man would be Gordon Langdon.

RON MARSHALL Like the others, a fluent deliverer of the bowl. His main attribute though, was his calmness under pressure. You always had the feeling that Ron was on top of every situation. Although dogged by bad health for many years, Ron proved himself an all-rounder by winning the Australian singles title and representing Australia as a skipper.

BOB MIDDLETON A World Bowls winner of bronze and silver medals, Bob is in my estimate, among the best slow-green players in the country. Over the years he has chalked up a long list of victories in Victorian championships and tournaments, but has lacked the opportnities to enhance these outside the state. Since his 'comeback' in 1980, Bob has maintained his class on the slow greens, and proved equally adept on all surfaces.

ALBERT NEWTON One of the all-time greats, Albert is a master tactician, always on the lookout for that delicate trail or fast drive to demoralise his opponents. His dedication to the sport, his physical fitness and smooth delivery have helped Albert to stay at the top far longer than most other bowlers.

ROB PARRELLA Colourful and dynamic are not the adjectives usually associated with lawn bowlers, but they certainly fit Parella. His is the type of personality needed in the game. Always a bundle of energy, Rob formerly represented Australia at Bocce, which probably accounts for his extremely accurate and powerful driving skills. Yet he blends these skills with an amazing ability to follow a drive with an equally accurate draw-shot, one of the hardest combinations to play. Rob has a keen and alert mind, and is flexible enough to change tactics when down, making him one of the best fighters playing bowls today.

KEITH POOLE A team player of the first order and one of nature's gentlemen. Yet I cannot help but think that Keith's outstanding record might have been even greater, but for what some people might regard as the flaw of being friendly with his rivals. Keith's high standard of sporting conduct is such that it has the effect of 'lifting' his opponents and this is particularly evident in his international appearances. May his tribe increase.

FRANK SOARS A great all-rounder, Frank impressed with his will to win, or if you like, his killer instinct. In the decade up to 1975, Frank had no peer as a singles player and a fours skipper; and he absolutely exuded confidence.

DUNCAN TAYLOR Has confined his bowls to teams play for some years now, which is a pity because Duncan has been a state singles winner and a state Champion of Champions. In draw-shot play, he rates as one of this country's most consistent over the past twenty years. In fact, to my knowledge, he has no peer as a number two and has played more than 200 games for his state, mostly in that position.

TREVOR WAGNER If confidence is what is looked for in a bowler, then Trevor is our man. With a smooth delivery and an excellent judge of pace, he excells on a fast green and is one of the hardest men to beat in a single-handed game.

CLARRIE WATKINS A good singles player, but to me, the most outstanding skipper in Australia. Clarrie is a believer in the theory that a captain should lead by example. He has all the shots and excells in playing each bowl at the correct pace to give maximum results. I have never seen Clarrie ruffled and I know that he always gets the best from his team.

DON WOOLNOUGH Don edges out Queenslanders Bob Purcell and Stan Coomber as the best leader in my time. The proof lies in Don's record of silver and bronze medals at the World Championships in South Africa, and his effort in representing Victoria in the lead position on more than 300 occasions. His concentration and application are outstanding, and any young player could learn a great deal by observing the 'master leader', Don Woolnough.

GLOSSARY

This book has, I hope, been written in such a way that the meaning is clear. Like any sport however, lawn bowls has its own special jargon; and for those who want to know how some of these words and phrases fit into the pattern of the game, I append the most commonly used.

BACKHAND Bowl delivered with the large identifying disc on the outside. For the right-hander, that is on the left.

BACKWOOD Bowls nearest the ditch — often so placed as 'insurance' against the jack being moved to the rear. Also known as the 'back-est' bowl.

BANK The raised area behind the ditch

BIAS 'Weighted' or small disc side of the bowl which causes it to turn in an arc. Deliver the bowl with the small disc facing the wrong side and it will turn away from, instead of towards, the target. This is known as 'wrong bias'. Don't do it; it may cost you drinks all round.

BLOCK SHOT Bowl placed in direct line between the mat and the jack.

BOUNDARY The rink area is defined by an imaginary line down either side, drawn the length of the green between the boundary pegs. The backboard behind the end ditches is also defined as the boundary of the rink.

BURNT END Canadian/American term for a dead end.

CANT Bowl turned slightly in the hand against the bias. Also known as tilt.

DEAD BOWL Unless it is a toucher, any bowl which finishes outside the rink is dead. A toucher, however, remains 'live' if it finishes in the ditch inside the boundary lines.

DEAD END If the jack is moved outside the imaginary lines between the boundary pegs, then the end is 'dead' and should be replayed.

In some local rules, however, a 'dead' end may not be replayed, as a means of saving time.

DITCH The 'gutter' at each end of the green.

DRAW or *DRAW-SHOT* Bowl delivered to finish in a specific position.

DRIVE Bowl delivered at a very fast pace. In England, it can be called a firing shot.

END Started by rolling the jack, and finished when each bowler has delivered the required number of bowls and the score decided.

FOOT-FAULT When the rule governing feet on the mat and delivery are contravened. Remember that your rear foot must be on or above the mat as the bowl is released.

GRASS or *GREEN* Term used to describe the line or path a bowl takes. To take more grass means to bowl out wider.

HEAD This is formed by the jack and the bowls drawn to and around it.

JACK The small white 'ball' — the aim of the game being to deliver your bowls as near as possible to it. The number of bowls you have nearer the jack than the closest bowls of your opponent is your score for that end.

JACK HIGH Looking from the mat, the front surfaces of the bowl and the jack are level.

JACK LOW A New Zealand term meaning short of jack high.

LEADER The first player to deliver in a game of pairs, triples or fours.

MARKER The person who assists singles players by setting up the jack after it is rolled. He also scores and answers players' questions about the position of the head.

MEASURER The third player in fours, and the second in triples. One of his tasks is to measure for shot in a close head.

PLANT Two bowls close together and lined up

94

with the jack or a particular bowl. Sometimes called a 'set', or in Queensland, a 'charlie'.

RINK The playing area. See 'Boundary'.

RUNNING SHOT Bowl delivered with sufficient speed to reach the ditch. Also known as a 'reaching' shot, or 'upshot' or 'onshot'.

SECOND The second player to deliver in triples or fours. His other specified task is to keep the scorecard and scoreboard in fours.

SKIPPER The captain and last player in teams matches.

SHOTS UP The number of bowls nearer the jack than your opponent's nearest.

SHOTS DOWN The reverse, and hardly the best position.

TAKE OUT Remove an opposition bowl with a drive or on-shot.

TOUCHER A bowl that has touched the jack and remained within the rink boundaries. When the skipper applies white chalk to your bowl, you will know you have a toucher!

TRAIL SHOT Bowl delivered in such a way as to move the jack a short distance.

UMPIRE The adjudicator in disputes, close measures, bowls or jack out of bounds etc.

WEIGHT The amount of thrust applied to a bowl or jack in delivery.

WHIP Exaggerated turn of the bowl, usually caused by wind.

WRESTING SHOT Bowl delivered above draw-weight to push an opponent's bowl through and take its place. A 'wresting toucher' finishes against the jack.